STAFF
DEVELOPMENT

ALA Editions purchases fund advocacy, awareness, and accreditation programs for library professionals worldwide.

STAFF DEVELOPMENT

A PRACTICAL GUIDE | FOURTH EDITION

Edited by

Andrea Wigbels Stewart,

Carlette Washington-Hoagland,

and Carol T. Zsulya

Prepared by the Staff Development Committee, Human Resources Section,
Library Leadership and Management Association

An imprint of the American Library Association
Chicago | 2013

Andrea Wigbels Stewart is interim university librarian at The Gelman Library, George Washington University. She received her master's degree in education and human development from George Washington University's Graduate School of Education and Human Development. Andrea served as LLAMA's HRS section secretary and cochair of the Staff Development Committee.

Carlette Washington-Hoagland is coordinator of staff development and diversity programming at the University of Iowa Libraries. Her research interests include staff development, usability testing, service quality, engagement, sexual harassment, and retention. Carlette holds an MA in library and information science from the University of Iowa and an MS in sociology from Iowa State University.

Carol T. Zsulya is head, collection management, the business/economics librarian, and communication librarian at Cleveland State University. Carol received an MSLS degree from Case Western Reserve University. She has participated in several programs of recent Charleston Conferences on e-books and technology's impact on academic libraries.

Printed in the United States of America

17 16 15 14 13   5 4 3 2 1

Extensive effort has gone into ensuring the reliability of the information in this book; however, the publisher makes no warranty, express or implied, with respect to the material contained herein.

ISBNs: 978-0-8389-1149-5 (paper); 978-0-8389-9623-2 (PDF). For more information on digital formats, visit the ALA Store at alastore.ala.org and select eEditions.

Library of Congress Cataloging-in-Publication Data
Staff development : a practical guide. — Fourth edition / prepared by the Staff Development
    Committee, Human Resources Section, Library Leadership and Management Association;
    edited by Andrea Stewart, Carlette Washington-Hoagland, and Carol Zsulya.
  pages cm
    Includes bibliographical references and index.
    ISBN 978-0-8389-1149-5 (pbk. : alk. paper)
    1. Library employees—In-service training. 2. Library education (Continuing education)
  3. Library personnel management. 4. Career development. I. Stewart, Andrea.
  II. Washington-Hoagland, Carlette. III. Zsulya, Carol. IV. Library Leadership and
  Management Association. Human Resources Section. Staff Development Committee.
  Z668.5.S7 2013
  023'.8—dc23   2012010062

Cover design by Casey Bayer. Cover image © Igor Kisselev/Shutterstock, Inc.
Text design by Kimberly Thornton in Mercury Text, Vista Sans, and Vista Slab.

♾ This paper meets the requirements of ANSI/NISO Z39.48-1992 (Permanence of Paper).

Contents

Introduction to the Fourth Edition

HUMAN RESOURCES, OUR STAFF, ARE ONE OF THE MOST IM-portant resources libraries possess in the changing information world. Today, with limited fiscal resources and new technological innovations, libraries—whether academic, public, or special—are facing great challenges as they work toward meeting their missions and enhancing the institutions or communities they belong to. Staff development and training are not only important; they are essential if libraries are to meet these challenges and add value.

This fourth edition of *Staff Development: A Practical Guide* was challenging to produce, for many reasons. The third edition of this guide was published in 2001. As the editors tackled the production of this new edition, we recognized that many themes, though still important to include, needed updating and a new focus. Many changes in technology and library human resource management drove our decisions to add several new chapters, such as "The Strategic Imperative of Library Staff Development," "Cross-Functional Training and Collaboration in the Organization," and "Leading from Any Position."

All three editors served as chair or cochair of the Library Leadership and Management Association's (LLAMA) Human Resources Section (HRS) Staff

Development Committee while planning and editing this publication. This new edition would not have been possible without the ongoing support of the committee members we worked with. Many of them contributed chapters and advice along the way.

No single publication can provide all the information and tools that human resource professionals need, so we encourage readers to attend LLAMA HRS Staff Development Committee programs, preconferences, and conferences.

Andrea W. Stewart
Carlette Washington-Hoagland
Carol T. Zsulya

Part I

Building a Staff Development Program

Elaine Z. Jennerich and Lisa A. Oberg

chapter 1 /
Introduction to Staff Development

N 1988 A SMALL TOME APPEARED WITH PRACTICAL ADVICE ABOUT STAFF development in libraries (Lipow, 1988). It was one of the only guides available that addressed the practicalities of a fledgling area of interest. The literature about staff development continues to remain relatively small in the library world, but there is no dearth of content in other fields. From authors who are public school educators to corporate trainers and consultants, one can find copious amounts of development-related content in virtually any format.

In the span of the three editions of this book, technologies, jargon, and fads have come and gone. In the second edition, Lipow's (1992) chapter on visual aids included the preparation and use of transparency overheads, easels and flip charts, 35 mm slides, handouts, and exactly three sentences about computer presentation software, which "require special (sometimes expensive) hardware and software and considerable practice before they can be used" (p. 71). By the time of the third edition, in 2001, online tutorials, websites, use of a laptop for demos, and HTML-based presentations appeared. In this fourth edition, an entire chapter is devoted to online tool options such as wikis, blogs, and social networking communities. Robert Pirsig (1974), author of *Zen and the Art of Motorcycle Maintenance: An Inquiry into Values*, said, "Technology presumes there's just one right way to do things and there never is" (p. 166).

Hence, we find the proliferation of more "right" ways to do things, including staff development things.

From 1988 on, there have also been developments in the theoretical constructs that underlie some areas of staff development. Staff development practitioners reengineered almost everything, created learning organizations, developed client-centered libraries, planned strategically, adopted process improvement techniques, created cultures of change, conducted needs and climate assessments, coached and mentored for results, transferred learning, and delved into many of the tools in the field of organization development. Working through such ideological and pragmatic exercises is a good thing, because it requires that we question what we and staff want to achieve and why.

Sounds pretty sophisticated and complex, doesn't it? That's why the content in this book is so useful. It assumes that you have an interest in staff development because you (or a committee or the director) want to start or improve a program. It also assumes that you need the basics, want to sound somewhat knowledgeable about the subject, and are looking to get some practical ideas. You may also want a launching pad for further study. This book can certainly help in all those ways!

So, what is this thing called staff development? Staff development is change. It is not capital-C change. It is an amalgam of small changes that take place in the behavior of individual staff members, which in turn can affect the whole team or unit or organization positively. For example:

- A team leader begins to provide an agenda the day before a meeting.
- The library director decides to stop by an employee's desk and say thanks.
- A staff member starts to read and answer e-mail daily.
- A junior staff member speaks up for the first time in a meeting.
- Two staff members who have been getting together for coffee for years invite a third to come along.
- A truly difficult employee becomes less strident.
- A rather shy staff member volunteers to be a new employee's orientation "buddy."

Change will not take place overnight, and the results generally accrue over the long term rather than immediately.

You might be thinking, "You mean that if our library creates a staff development program, based on a well-done needs assessment, using a variety of proven methods and technologies, all we get out of it are small changes? And we probably won't be able to 'fix' all our personnel problems, and it will take time?" Yes—and the good news is that each small behavior change means that the library has created an environment in which staff members feel comfortable enough to change. The team leader who uses an agenda finds that meetings become more productive and easier to facilitate. The director discovers that appreciating and recognizing individual staff members is a powerful management tool and garners cooperation. Reading and answering e-mail shows that the employee has taken personal responsibility for communication. The junior staff member feels that his or her opinions and suggestions are valued. The coffee mates have expanded their network. The stress levels of the people who work with the less strident staff member are a bit lower. The shy staff member feels the need to engage more with others. Behavior change may be the result of a workshop or class, reading, coaching, modeling, or a combination of those. In any case, small changes in behavior often make big differences in outcomes.

It is the belief of all of us who have contributed to this edition that the advantages of instituting and improving staff development programs far outweigh the disadvantages. In terms of advantages, most importantly, staff development is tangible evidence to employees that they are valued and worth the investment in time and resources. There is significant merit in naming any effort or program developed to support your organization's mission, goals, and staff. As a selling point, it is useful in hiring and retention. It empowers staff to learn new skills and encourages them to share what they've learned with others. Staff training and development programs can build morale, furnish opportunities for professional growth and cross-training, and provide structure for communication and organizational change.

Having an active staff development program takes the pressure off asking, "Who is going to offer this?" or "To whom should I send my training or development idea?" By setting goals and objectives for learning, the staff development can send a common message throughout the organization. An excellent example is customer service. Developing a customer service philosophy and policy and then teaching staff the appropriate hard and soft skills sets the stage for improved performance for in-person and virtual services.

Depending on the size of your program, it may provide funding for staff training and other programs that benefit both the individual and the organization. Often staff members learn to anticipate challenges and barriers to progress and are eager to produce solutions. An exciting outcome of staff training and development is a positive do-it-yourself (DIY) attitude. For example, staff members can learn to design and execute a planning retreat, successfully brainstorm new ways to serve customers, volunteer for committees or other team assignments, or mentor new employees. The reason for the DIY attitude is that staff development provides employees with specific tools (e.g., facilitation techniques, idea generation, planning strategies). Staff members can learn to use those tools in various ways, such as observation, practice in appropriate situations, coaching, and classroom instruction. Once learned, the tools are useful in a variety of situations.

There can be disadvantages associated with having a staff training and development program. Staff may expect the staff development program to direct and monitor all their learning and professional development. They may expect formal training to be offered for every job-related task rather than jumping in and learning on their own. Conversely, employees who have learned new skills may feel confident and empowered to leave the organization and seek new challenges. For some staff, the "development" part of training and development is considered inappropriate. "Just teach me the technical skills I need to get the job done," they say. "I don't want to be developed!" Long-term supervisors and managers may have an especially difficult time dealing with changing expectations for how they direct and work with their teams. If the organization determines that some aspects of the staff training and development program are required rather than voluntary, some complaining will probably ensue.

The organization may view staff development as a catchall for all training needs, which can lead to lack of ownership for some types of very specialized training. Not all training is appropriately offered as staff development, and doing so can create some tension and may require negotiation. Staff development programs can require funding, even if it is simply in the form of in-kind contributions of time. A successful program leads to higher expectations among staff members for an even better and expanded program. It is important to note, however, that staff development is not simply a training program for adopting technology innovations; rather, a robust program includes both soft and hard skills to help advance the organization's employees.

From single-purpose to multitiered to broad, comprehensive programs aimed to change organizational culture, staff development programs should evolve and change over time to meet both current and future need. Regardless of how small or large your program is, something is better than nothing, and there is a value in naming any program, training session, or discussion group as an activity in support of staff training and development. Remember, as in all things, results take time, so include assessment and benchmarks in planning as a way to measure your success. In addition, staff development can lead to changing expectations on both sides, which is an outward sign that your organization is evolving.

Change is a cornerstone of today's workplace. Having an infrastructure in place to support change enables staff to more actively participate in the change personally and in groups. An active program creates a forum for an organization to respond to changes more quickly. In flexible organizations with environments in which employees feel comfortable enough to change, the effect on morale is positive, which ultimately strengthens the organization and encourages future growth.

REFERENCES

Lipow, A. G. (Ed.). (1988). *Staff Development: A Practical Guide*. Chicago, IL: Library Administration and Management Association, American Library Association.

Lipow, A. G., Carver, D. A. (Eds.), & Library Administration and Management Association Staff Development Committee. (1992). *Staff Development: A Practical Guide* (2nd ed.). Chicago, IL: American Library Association.

Pirsig, R. (1974). *Zen and the Art of Motorcycle Maintenance: An Inquiry into Values*. New York, NY: Morrow.

Jeanne F. Voyles and Robyn Huff-Eibl

chapter 2

Needs Assessment
Planning, Implementation, and Action

N THE PAST DECADE THERE HAS BEEN INCREASED PRESSURE ON LI-
brary organizations to maintain or cut costs while increasing both
the variety and the quality of services offered. Additional resource
limitations and declining budgets have created an environment in
which organizations must focus on the services that bring value to
users in supporting their need for information, research, and education. Whether you agree with or dispute using the word *customer*,
we all work to meet the needs of our institutions and the communities we
serve. Needs assessment and the resulting services, measures, and outcomes
provide accountability for institutions, state and city government, accrediting
associations, and governing boards. As a result, needs assessment, evaluation,
measurement, and planning have become processes that are critical to organizational survival and success.

Needs assessment provides organizations with insight into existing services and whether to add, modify, or discontinue these services. Evaluation
provides organizations with knowledge of user satisfaction, effectiveness, and
efficiency. Together, needs assessment and evaluation are tools that allow for
data-based planning and decision making. Needs assessment and evaluation
are not onetime efforts. For organizations to envision current and future needs
successfully, they need to understand the importance of developing a culture

of continual needs assessment and evaluation (Lakos & Phipps, 2004). User needs and expectations are rapidly changing. We can no longer assume that we know what is best for our customers without asking them. Creating a climate of assessment allows organizations to keep up with changing user expectations. The purpose of needs assessment and evaluation is continuous improvement, the ability to meet user needs, and the ability to demonstrate and communicate the value of libraries.

For libraries to ensure successful delivery of services in a rapidly changing environment, they can use a variety of assessment tools and approaches to collect data and gather information from customers. These data can then be used to support the organization in its strategic planning process, which plans for new services, enhances or changes existing services, and plans for the abandonment of services that customers no longer need so that resources for new initiatives can be reallocated. As organizations, we also need to be proactive in scanning the environment and to be knowledgeable about changes, often to technology, that we can implement at our libraries.

This chapter presents a variety of methods that support a coordinated approach to planning, performance measurement, and accountability. All the methods and approaches presented have been implemented at the University of Arizona Library (UAL). At the University of Arizona there is a direct relationship between needs assessment and strategic planning. Our organization aligns needs assessment, strategic planning, team planning, individual planning, and performance management in one annual cycle of activities with a focus on customers and the future (see figure 2.1).

Figure 2.1: Continual Needs Assessment, Evaluation, and Planning

We share data and information obtained from our needs assessment with customers, student governance councils, student library advisory groups, and across the library for the benefit of other library teams. Our goal in communicating our value is to keep customers informed about changes that have resulted from their direct feedback and our work in scanning the environment.

Needs Assessment Data Gathering and Environmental Scanning Approaches

Each year at the University of Arizona our librarywide Strategic Long-Range Planning Team (SLRP) develops, distributes, and solicits feedback on a draft three- to five-year plan and identifies the critical few areas of focus for the upcoming year. Much of this plan is based on outcomes of needs assessment efforts and library or team environmental scans. Key groups, such as administrators, the SLRP team, and the director of project management and needs assessment, engage in dialogue about the critical few areas and how to make significant strategic progress during the upcoming year. The discussion includes a review of proposed librarywide and team-level projects that might be needed, critical areas that need to be addressed that may not be included in the proposed list of team projects, programs that could increase effectiveness by bringing related projects together, and teams that need to work together to accomplish the strategic or critical work identified.

At the team or department level, data gathered from needs assessment are also reviewed during the planning process. Each functional team creates its own strategic frameworks tied to the library's strategic plan. During team strategic-planning sessions, formal needs assessment data and feedback gathered throughout the year from customers are reviewed. The outcome of that team strategic-planning process is the creation or revision of quality standards pertaining to existing services and teams' identification of strategic and functional team projects to assist in the movement toward achieving three- to five-year goals. As part of the process other teams are often consulted when there are possibilities of collaboration in terms of cross-functional team projects.

Having a coordinated approach to needs assessment allows organizations to systematically bring in the voice of the customer. At UAL, these data are collected hourly, daily, and over the course of each fiscal year. Over time trend analysis is possible.

INTERNAL ASSESSMENT

Internal needs assessment collection includes the following:

- Online and in-person surveys
    LibQUAL Survey
    Action Gap Survey
    Library Report Card—library website form or e-mail used
        to collect positive and constructive feedback
- Feedback at the time of need or service
    customer feedback on completed digital projects
    tracking unmet customer needs using Desk Tracker soft-
        ware
- Usage statistics
- Project needs assessment or focus groups
- Observational data collection

EXTERNAL ASSESSMENT

We also use external sources to validate findings from internal data gathering. This adds to our overall environmental scanning process and helps us understand both the current situation and future trends. This includes the following:

- Keeping up to date on library publications and reports (e.g., *Horizon, Educause, Reference and User Services Quarterly*)
- Keeping up to date on changes and trends with library vendors, publishing, and so on
- Keeping up to date on changes in scholarly communication
- Participating in webinars
- Staff conference summaries
    librarians and staff: attend critical conferences, meetings,
        and workshops
    dean: reports what has been learned from conferences,
        meetings, and information collection from other libraries
- Participating in Listservs and benchmarking other institutions
- Participating in social networking or blogs

Although several staff assist in providing information and data for the team environmental scan document, key staff are assigned to specific areas to coordinate the overall process. In the Access and Information Services Team (AIST), four staff members are responsible for coordinating the AIST needs assessment, statistics, environmental scanning, and team planning processes. In addition:

- A library information analyst coordinates overall team environmental scanning, data collection and analysis, team statistics, and strategic planning processes (10 percent FTE).
- Three senior library information associates assist in coordination, and each is responsible for specific pieces (10 percent each FTE, with one who also manages team statistics at almost 20 percent FTE).
- A library information associate assists with data entry and running statistical reports from the integrated library system (5 percent FTE).

Overall, this accounts for 0.55 full-time equivalent (FTE) devoted to managing these processes. The scanners meet throughout the year with the AIST and the AIST's leadership team, composed of the team leader, four supervisors, and the library information analyst. Together the leadership team makes final decisions with the team scanners and input from the overall AIST team.

As data and information are collected, they are shared with various user groups, library teams (through team reports and the needs assessment librarian), and where appropriate with other libraries and consortia partners.

The following are examples of tools that can assist in the collection and collation of needs assessment data:

- NVivo (N6)—qualitative software created by QSR
- SurveyMonkey—quantitative and qualitative
- Excel (data and charts)—quantitative and charts
- LibPAS—library data management software created by Counting Opinions
- Desk Tracker

Then, AIST codes all user comments from the internal sources of data into twenty-five categories:

1. Service Point—Approachable
2. Service Point—Available
3. Service Point—General
4. Service Point—Knowledgeable
5. Database Issues
6. Library Collections
7. Missing Items
8. Software
9. Survey
10. Website
11. Code of Conduct
12. Computer Access
13. Environment
14. Hours
15. Meeting and Classroom Space
16. Security
17. Study Space
18. Account Issues
19. Claims Returned
20. Check-Ins
21. Equipment
22. Holds
23. Loan Policies
24. Loaner Laptops
25. Notices

Dimensions were added to these twenty-five categories by assigning neutral, negative, or positive tone. We used Strauss and Corbin's (1990) grounded theory approach to coding to develop the categories, as well as their axial coding to refine and define core categories.

All qualitative data are entered into NVivo. The comments are then coded for demographics—university status, gender, and discipline (if available). NVivo is a tool that allows us to analyze qualitative data using cross-tabulation or text searches or just to explore categories for a particular hypothesis. Twice per year, we provide an overview of our team data to AIST and the library's Strategic Planning Team. Once we start to see certain themes or concepts emerging, we analyze all data sets for that hypothesis. Sometimes we are asked to provide analysis on categories as needed.

CONSORTIA

There are multiple data sources to consider when gathering information and data. At UAL we often consult with colleagues at other libraries, consortia groups, or institutions that we consider progressive and forward thinking. We often ask whether our colleagues have completed any recent needs assessment of similar topics. Approaches in working with consortium partners can be through informal questions posted on Listservs or more formal surveys completed by member libraries. The responses from the Listserv and surveys provide useful information and data to guide libraries in making decisions from changing or creating a policy to planning for future or new services. Consortium partners are also a good resource for determining whether others have completed a similar needs assessment tool. To save time and resources, consider how you might modify and adapt another institution's assessment tool for your institution. Consortium members also provide an excellent opportunity to test or pilot a survey with a few colleagues. Consortium members often make a commitment to one another to respond promptly to member inquiries. Do not overlook the valuable resource in partnerships and consortia.

SURVEYS

Often surveys are the most popular approach to needs assessment. In taking this approach to gathering feedback, libraries must consider coordinating these efforts in their library. Often faculty, staff, and students are inundated with or unresponsive to surveys because of the volume they receive on a regular basis and the amount of time it takes to complete surveys. When considering a survey approach, think about whether the survey is too general, too long, or too specific. For very specific surveys, consider what your target audience will be that can best respond to the survey and provide you with data and information. Consider a random sample of a targeted population to survey. Often the most difficult component of creating a customer survey is asking the right questions. When creating surveys, do not assume that you know what customers need or how satisfied they are with a service.

Here is an approach that the University of Arizona's Document Delivery Team (DDT) used to assess customer satisfaction. In 2006 the DDT surveyed faculty, staff, and students on their satisfaction with interlibrary-loan journal

Figure 2.2: Action Gap Survey

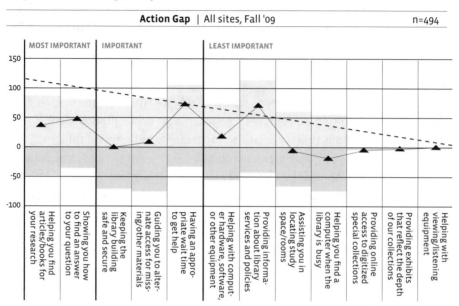

Looking at this chart, the biggest gap between the target (dashed line) and our performance (triangles) is "Keeping the building safe and secure." This would become an area of focus in the team planning process.

borrowing for article requests. Up until that point we had received positive comments from customers and little negative feedback. With the increased demands for interlibrary loan, research, and faster delivery of materials, the DDT decided to embark on a strategic project to assess the service quality and cost of filling interlibrary loan requests to borrow journal articles. For this project, the DDT designed a customer satisfaction survey and identified a target audience to receive the survey. The team received a high rate of return on the survey, and responses identified some specific needs of UAL customers. As a result of feedback, the DDT targeted turnaround time for improvement. A follow-up survey was administered in 2007 to faculty, staff, and students. The findings of that survey indicated that customer expectations were being met and that the service often exceeded expectations.

It is important to note that satisfaction surveys are often used but not always meaningful. When assessing customer satisfaction, an alternative to satisfaction surveys is a survey instrument called Action Gap, created by Cravenho and Sandvig (2003). This survey measures services on three dimensions:

Figure 2.3: The Balanced Scorecard Framework

what is most important to customers, what we do best, and what we need to improve. The information on this survey allows the institution to measure the gap between what needs the most improvement and the institution's target as ranked by customer importance (see figure 2.2). The benefit of using this survey instrument is ensuring that we focus efforts on areas that customers have identified as most important and as needing improvement. This is not always evident from a satisfaction survey.

UAL recently purchased LibPAS (Library Performance Assessment System), from Counting Opinions, and the system has the capability to handle both quantitative and qualitative data sets, all in one piece of software. In addition, LibPAS has the potential to enhance productivity and advocacy as a data-gathering, reporting, and management system.

Needs assessment data gathering and environmental scanning allow organizations to gain information that is useful in the creation and measurement of service goals. Using the Balanced Scorecard provides a measurement framework (Kaplan & Norton, 1996a, 1996b; see figure 2.3).

PERFORMANCE MEASURES RELATING TO CUSTOMERS

- *Outcome*: result for customers, gain for them, or the capability or benefit they will acquire; can be measured by, for example, customer retention, customer satisfaction, market share, and pre- and post-measures of ability or desired difference
- *Output*: amount of products; extent of services
- *Quality*: the qualitative outcome as judged by the customer; attributes or characteristics of the service, product, or outcome that the customer values and expects
- *Tangibles*: appearance of physical facilities, equipment, personnel, and communication materials
- *Reliability*: ability to perform the promised service dependably and accurately
- *Availability*: ability to access the service or receive the product when needed
- *Responsiveness*: willingness to help customers and provide prompt service; response time
- *Assurance*: knowledge and courtesy of employees and their ability to convey trust and confidence
- *Empathy*: caring, individualized attention that the firm provides its customers
- *Self-reliance*: the ability to work in a self-directed way; work on one's own; self-navigate; product is easily accessible with on-demand service

PERFORMANCE MEASURES FOR EXTERNAL STAKEHOLDERS AND FUNDING AGENCIES

- *ROI*: return on investment, or the most bang for your buck; economic value added
- *Employee productivity improvement*: output produced compared to employee compensation (return on compensation)
- *Unit costs*: costs per unit of output or per transaction
- *Cost reduction*: reduced costs with same or increased value to customers
- *Cost per customer*: cost of service per customers served
- *Expansion of customer base*: increase in actual customers served from potential customer base

- *Expansion of products and services within funding limitations*: new products or services that increase agency value to customers

PERFORMANCE MEASURES RELATING TO INTERNAL BUSINESS PROCESSES
- *Cycle-time reduction*: from receipt of request to customer delivery without affecting quality
- *Accuracy*: reduction in number of errors per total output
- *Quality*: quality as judged by the capability of the process
- *Product quality*: increase in readability or usability of output, level of reliability of output, and so on
- *Accessibility*: increase in product or service accessibility
- *Communication*: increase in information about the availability of a service and its usefulness to customers

PERFORMANCE MEASURES RELATING TO LEARNING AND GROWTH
- Employee's satisfaction and information system availability
- Skills and abilities acquired and opportunity for practice or application of skills
- Opportunity for feedback that supports growth
- Employee support for time and effort
- Agreement on expectations

At UAL, teams create quality standards to measure success of our products and services. The library uses a variety of measures from the four balanced scorecard categories. Data gathered from these measures feed into the ongoing assessment activities at UAL.

Conclusion

Organizations can use a variety of methods, from simple to complex, to assess customers' needs. Integration of needs assessment and strategic planning in the organization is critical for ensuring that libraries are progressing in the right direction. With the fast pace of our changing environments, organizations need to be agile enough to make the necessary changes in services, technology, and their approaches to meet the needs of customers, needs that are essential to customers' research, education, and lifelong learning. Results of needs assessment can tell us where we have been successful and can indicate new areas and services to focus on in the future.

REFERENCES

Cravenho, J., & Sandvig, B. (2003). "Survey for Action, Not Satisfaction." *Quality Progress, 36*(3), 63–68.

Kaplan, R. S., & Norton, D. P. (1996a). *The Balanced Scorecard: Translating Strategy into Action.* Boston, MA: Harvard Business School Press.

Kaplan, R. S., & Norton, D. P. (1996b). "Using the Balanced Scorecard as a Strategic Management System." *Harvard Business Review, 74*(1), 75–85.

Lakos, A., & Phipps, S. (2004). "Creating a Culture of Assessment: A Catalyst for Organizational Change." *Portal: Libraries and the Academy, 4*(3), 345–361.

Strauss, A. L., & Corbin, J. M. (1990). *Basics of Qualitative Research: Grounded Theory Procedures and Techniques.* Newbury Park, CA: Sage.

ADDITIONAL RESOURCES

Dols, L., Knight, E., & Voyles, J. F. (2009). "Interlibrary Loan Meets Customer Expectations: The University of Arizona Library's Experience in Applying Six Sigma Process Improvement." *Journal of Interlibrary Loan, Document Delivery and Electronic Reserve, 19*(1), 75–94.

Dudden, R. F. (2007). *Using Benchmarking, Needs Assessment, Quality Improvement, Outcome Measurement, and Library Standards.* New York, NY: Neal-Schuman.

Hernon, P., & McClure, C. R. (1990). *Evaluation and Library Decision Making.* Norwood, NJ: Ablex.

Library Assessment Conference. (2006, 2008, 2010). "Building Effective, Sustainable, Practical Assessment." Retrieved from www.libraryassessment.org

Matthews, J. R. (2004). *Measuring for Results: The Dimensions of Public Library Effectiveness.* Westport, CT: Libraries Unlimited.

Raynna Bowlby and Linda Plunket

chapter 3

The Strategic Imperative of Library Staff Development

Staff Development and Library Strategic Planning

REFLECT, FOR A MOMENT, ON A LIBRARY STRATEGIC PLAN. IT IS A set of aspirations for the future through which the library articulates its intention to continuously progress in fulfilling its core mission. A strategic plan emphasizes activities that will anticipate and satisfy the needs and wants of the library's users today and in the envisioned future. A library's strategic plan describes its aims for a variety of essential user services, from efficient and effective customer service transactions to individually focused consultations and public programming. It stresses appropriate collections—print, digital, and multimedia—depending on the community's needs and preferences. Today's strategic plan likely also addresses how the library can use new technologies to enhance the user experience or increase access to its unique special and archival materials, as well as its shared networked resources. The strategic plan also considers how to align library buildings and facilities with contemporary user behaviors in regard to individual study and social interactions. In summary, an effective plan includes strategic agendas that are based on fulfilling the user-centered mission of the organization. Likewise, any future-oriented plans and goals related to library staff must be aligned with and must support the organization in fulfilling its mission and evolving vision. The rationale for including goals addressing library staff development in the strategic plan is, quite simply, that to do so is strategic.

Staff development, also referred to as employee development, "is the system of providing opportunities for employees within an organization to reach their full potential (through improving skills and competency) and become of greater value to the organization" (Heery & Noon, 2008). Similarly, human resource development has been described as "learning at the individual, group and organizational levels to enhance the effectiveness of human resources with the purpose of achieving the objectives of the organization" (Wilson, 2005). None other than management guru Peter Drucker (1999) exhorts us to consider the strategic imperative of our human resources, stating that "knowledge work requires continuous learning on the part of the knowledge worker" and that to be successful, the knowledge work must be focused as part of a system, on the needs of the customer and business strategy (p. 142). What is foremost in including staff development in the library's strategic plan, then, is to establish and reinforce a sound philosophy about the effective use of staff resources in the organization and the need to continuously change and develop for the future of the organization and its service to customers. Organizational leaders and managers of staff must provide information about the knowledge, skills, and abilities needed for the organization to be successful in the present and the future and must provide opportunities and a supportive environment for individuals to develop.

Staff development is not strategic when it is employed primarily in reactive and episodic ways. For example, when a library introduces new technology, a training session may respond to a particular need for some specific knowledge and skill in the library in order to use the system correctly. Such onetime or periodic training is requisite for effective performance. But if this is the sole area of learning, then it implies that the effort is for the successful implementation of the technology, not necessarily for the development of the staff. At the other end of the spectrum, staff development is not strategic when we allow it to become "all about us." Often, one or more goals about staff development are included in the library's strategic plan with the intention of addressing staff morale or indicating that the library "values the staff." However, this places the emphasis on the wrong end and neglects the truly essential nature of the staff and its continual learning and development in support of the organization's mission. As Barham, Frazer, and Heath (1988) noted:

People, of course, are far and away the most important resource in any company. But they are not more than that. It is very easy to forget when endeavoring to develop people and to care for them, and even to love them that the needs of the business must come first. Without that, there can be no lasting security. A fool's paradise in which effort is concentrated only on the present well-being of the staff, without regard for the future, will eventually disintegrate and it may well be the staff that suffer most. (p. 28)

Staff development is strategic when it enables staff to create a user-centered library, encourages staff to anticipate continuous change, and enhances staff capabilities in areas identified as key to the future of the organization.

Staff Development in Support of Library Users

Building on this theme, then, a user-centered library considers staff development a strategic investment. Christensen (2006) notes that "development is an investment in building behaviors that result in successful performance" (pp. 172–173). A library that pursues a strategy of staff development as an investment will be motivated by the principle that the organization exists to provide benefit to its community of users and that the expertise of the staff is one of the ways that the library supports users.

Westport (CT) Public Library Strategic Plan: Engaging the Community, Building for the Future, 2007–2010

The Westport Public Library (see www.docstoc.com/docs/41490076/Westport -Public-Library-Strategic-Plan) identifies staff development that will benefit the support of users, indicating that one strategic issue is "investment in staff":

"The Library provides its staff with the training and with the opportunities for professional development necessary to keep services both relevant and excellent."

"Library staff have become information navigators for Library users. To meet its commitment to provide the excellent service expected by the community, the Library must provide the staff with ongoing technical training and customer-oriented skills development."

University Libraries, Loyola University Chicago Strategic Plan, 2010–2013

The Loyola University Libraries expresses the rationale for and actions that will lead to success in implementing the strategy (see http://libraries.luc.edu/sites/all/attachments/LibrariesStrategicPlan.pdf):

RATIONALE

"Increase the impact of the libraries' subject services including collection development and specialized reference and instruction services. All of our services focuses on the success of the academic mission, and the subject specialist librarians have primary responsibility for ensuring that the libraries fully support what is being taught and researched at Loyola. Subject specialists will also be necessary to ensure Loyola's Centers of Excellence have access to the library resources required to develop their multi-disciplinary programs. Through increased communication and collaboration, we can recognize, develop, and deliver the most relevant collections and services."

ACTION

"Develop individualized professional development plans for subject specialists to deepen their expertise in relevant areas of knowledge, including the academic disciplines for which they select, the structure of scholarly communication in those disciplines, specialized research tools and methods, digital resource creation, and new information technology."

Staff Development for Continuous Change

Another strategic imperative for library staff development is the impact of rapid and unrelenting change that is affecting libraries. Change of this magnitude heightens the critical importance of continuous learning and recurrent retooling of staff. Peter Vaill (1996) describes the turbulence and change in organizations as an environment of "continual newness," as "permanent white water" (p. xiv). "Nonstop white water puts individuals in the position of doing things they have little experience with or have never done before" and it requires "continual learning under constantly changing conditions" (Vaill, 1996, p. 19). In this environment, library staff must perform effectively today and be preparing to perform effectively in the future, for whatever the future has in store. Indeed, some of the work that staff must attend to today is unlikely to be needed, or to be a priority for staff time and effort, in the future. The strategic library will plan for the retooling of staff so that some work is deemphasized and so that staff resources will be directed toward new priorities.

Creating the 21st Century for NYU: Our Strategic Plan
2007–2012

New York University Library identifies staff development for continuous learning and retooling as one of ten strategic goals and elaborates several key actions; furthermore, the plan presents a "visionary scenario" that projects how this goal and its associated actions will be enacted by individual staff and leaders of the organization (see http://library.nyu.edu/about/Strategic_Plan.pdf):

"Use recruitment, promotion, mentoring, and professional development to build a workforce that meets the requirements of the 21st century library."

{SELECTED} KEY ACTIONS

"Create comprehensive professional development programs that ensure that staff at all levels will have the necessary tools, knowledge, and support to achieve our strategic goals."

"Develop a collaborative program (drawing on potential from all library departments) devoted to the identification of, and training in, the new skills necessary to accomplish our mission, thereby maximizing the opportunities for staff to assume new and different roles."

"Using the faculty mentoring for promotion process as a model, develop techniques that focus on individual growth and development and the creation of opportunities to contribute to the library's mission."

VISIONARY SCENARIO

"For the last few months staff member X has spent her monthly mentoring sessions with her department manager discussing the changes in libraries and their impact on her line position. Together they reach the conclusion that staff member X's present duties no longer reflect what is needed for the library of the 21st century and that new duties and systems need to be put in place. At the request of her supervisor, staff member X has had several sessions with IT members to discuss the new systems. She has also joined a forum and blog devoted to the new methods that she will need to employ. Next month staff member X will be visiting another academic institution where she can see the new process in action and discuss with staff there how they accomplished a smooth transition. She will also attend a class in SCPS to gain skills necessary for her new role. As a result of the joint decision, followed by careful preparation and in-depth training, staff member X is poised and eager to leave her old position behind and embrace a new method of delivering service."

Library Staff Development for Workforce Planning

Another strategic imperative of staff development relates to the availability of adequate human resources for libraries. There has been considerable documentation over the past decade about the "graying of the profession" (see www .bls.gov/oco/ocos068.htm#projections_data) and the impact that impending retirements may have on the ability of libraries to operate successfully. Particularly in the current economic environment, where hiring moratoria may impede the recruitment of new librarians into these vacancies, it becomes even more necessary—and strategic—to address the development of capabilities among existing staff.

Sault Ste. Marie Public Library: A Strategic Agenda 2003–2008

The Sault Ste. Marie Public Library presents succession planning as one of the strategic challenges it is facing and prepares a set of staff goals to use staff development for enhanced support of users and succession planning (see www.ssmpl.ca/uploads/docs/strat03to08.pdf):

CHALLENGES

Succession Planning
"The average age of the Sault Ste. Marie Public Library employee in 2003 is 48 years, while the median age is 50. The library will experience a significant turnover of staff within the next 5 to 10 years as the employees born into the 'baby-boom' generation reach their retirement age. Issues such as knowledge management transfer, development of core competencies, employee recruitment and staff development all need to be addressed."

Staff Goal
"The employees of the Sault Ste. Marie Public Library will continue to develop their skills and knowledge to provide high-quality library service that meets the needs of our patrons. To achieve this goal the Sault Ste. Marie Public Library will pursue strategies in the following areas:

1.   Provide the necessary tools and training to:
1.1. Enable staff to perform their jobs efficiently and effectively
1.2. Support the ongoing development of job skills
1.3. Enable staff to respond effectively to library patrons
1.4. Understand the impact of emerging technologies and implement them as required
3.   Redefining job functions
3.1. To enable more flexibility and to reflect the impact of changing technologies and shifts in library service priorities
3.2. Place more emphasis on critical job functions such as planning, analysis, evaluation, and problem solving."

Duke University Libraries: Connecting People + Ideas: A Strategic Plan for the Duke University Libraries 2006–2010

Duke University Libraries outlines the importance of workforce planning and corresponding activity to develop needed competencies with a strategy and the resources required (see http://library.duke.edu/about/planning/Perkins-Library -Strategic-Plan-2006-2010.pdf):

STRATEGY

"Develop and implement an effective workforce plan to create the optimal workforce for the Library's future and to identify appropriate workload staffing levels necessary for running current operations."

RESOURCES REQUIRED

"1) Use existing resources, from both the Library and Duke HR, to create a workforce plan by analyzing the composition of the current staff, forecasting anticipated needs and competencies, assessing the gap between our current and anticipated needs, and developing strategies for bridging the gap; 2) use an estimated $15,000 from Library restricted funds, to hire a consultant to facilitate the design and implementation of a succession planning system to address skill development in leadership, management, and critical staff positions; 3) use existing operating funds for training and staff development to ensure that staff develop the skills necessary to assume new roles; 4) emphasize management/supervisory training given the projected loss of middle managers to retirement during the time period of this plan."

The University of Arizona Libraries and the Center for Creative Photography: Strategic Plan 2008–2012

The University of Arizona Libraries and the Center for Creative Photography (CCP) considers the continuous identification of needed staff competencies and the ongoing presence of these to be important to the key result area of operational effectiveness, which is supported by a 3–5 year goal and quality standard (see http://intranet. library.arizona.edu/xf/slrp/documents/FY08-12StrategicPlanwithMeasures.pdf):

3–5 YEAR GOAL

"The UA Libraries and CCP have . . . [s]ystems in place which permit us to identify, maintain, develop, and/or acquire the competencies which staff need to deliver exceptional customer service in the future."

QUALITY STANDARD

"Plan (including development and use of competency-based position descriptions, succession plan to develop or acquire competencies and talent to replace losses from retirement or other attrition, and process and measure to assess whether Libraries and CCP possess the competencies and talent required to fulfill its mission) developed by June 30, 2008, and fully implemented by June 30, 2010."

Library Staff Development in the "Strategy-Focused Organization"

How can the impact of staff development be demonstrated? How can a library communicate to its stakeholders that an ongoing investment in staff development is essential? The fundamental importance of staff development to organizational strategy can be found by studying the Balanced Scorecard, a strategically focused planning methodology developed and enhanced since the early 1990s by Kaplan and Norton (see figure 2.3). The Balanced Scorecard "translates an organization's mission and strategy into a comprehensive set of performance measures that provides a framework for a strategic measurement and management system . . . the scorecard measures organizational performance across four balanced perspectives—financial, customer, internal business processes, and learning and growth." (Kaplan & Norton, 1996, p. 2)

Matthews (2008, p. 3) explains "the scorecard requires the organization to create a cause-and-effect relationship between the perspectives. For example, if a company invests in additional training for its staff and provides the necessary information technology infrastructure (the organizational readiness, or learning and growth, perspective), then the staff members will be better able to develop improvements in procedures and processes (the internal process . . . perspective) and thus work more productively. The staff will also be better able to respond to customer needs and requests, which will lead to more satisfied customers (the customer perspective), which in turn will lead to higher revenues or better profits (the financial perspective)."

Matthews (2008) maintains that in the not-for-profit arena of libraries, the financial perspective does not result from these other efforts, but is the starting point and that "financial and other resources provided to the library . . . ensure that skilled staff . . . are in place" (p. 21). He further clarifies that the learning and growth perspective "is designed to assess the library's ability to compete in the future. The organization may assess the skills of its employees to determine whether the right mix and depth of skills are present to meet the changing competitive environment" (Matthews, 2008, p. 3).

University of Virginia Balanced Scorecard

The University of Virginia has implemented the Balanced Scorecard (see http://www2.lib.virginia.edu/bsc/metrics/all0708.html#learning):

LEARNING/GROWTH PERSPECTIVE
"How well is the library positioned to expand our organizational capacity by creating an environment supportive of continuous personal and organizational development?"

GOAL
"Foster learning among its employees to encourage creativity, cooperation, and innovation."

IMPACT OF STAFF DEVELOPMENT
"Target 1: Positive scores (4 or 5) on 80% of responses to staff development statements in the biennial work-life survey."

"Target 2: Positive scores (4 or 5) on 60% of responses to staff development statements in the biennial work-life survey."

Note: Among the metrics used in the University of Virginia Library Worklife Survey include these related to staff development:

"I actively seek opportunities to learn new skills or improve my skills"

"My supervisor supports me in pursuing training and educational opportunities"

"There are adequate staff development opportunities provided by the Library"

"The quality of training I receive from the Library helps me to do my job better"

"The training offered by the Library is relevant to my job"

"I am trained for new responsibilities in a timely manner"

"I receive adequate support to attend workshops, conferences, and other learning opportunities outside of the Library and/or University" (http://www2.lib.virginia.edu/mis/reports)

The strategic imperative of staff development in libraries arises from a core philosophy that the library must be user-centered and continuously evolving to meet user needs, and consequently, that staff must be constantly acquiring new knowledge, skills, and abilities (competencies) in order to accomplish the organizational mission and meet current and future user needs. It is essential for library strategic plans to include a philosophy, vision, and goals related to staff development so that the overall human resource capacity of the organization will be strategically planned for and aligned.

REFERENCES

Barham, K., Frazer, J., & Heath, L. (1988). *Management for the Future: A Major Research Project Jointly Sponsored by the Foundation for Management Education and Ashridge Management College.* Berkhamsted, UK: Ashridge Management Research Group and Foundation for Management Education.

Christensen, R. (2006). *Roadmap to Strategic HR: Turning a Great Idea into a Business Reality.* New York, NY: AMACOM.

Drucker, P. F. (1999). *Management Challenges for the 21st Century.* New York, NY: Harper Business.

Heery, E., & Noon, M. (2008). *A Dictionary of Human Resource Management.* Oxford: Oxford University Press.

Kaplan, R. S., & Norton, D. P. (1996). *The Balanced Scorecard: Translating Strategy into Action.* Boston, MA: Harvard Business School Press.

Matthews, J. R. (2008). *Scorecard for Results: A Guide for Developing a Library Balanced Scorecard.* Westport, CT: Libraries Unlimited.

Vaill, P. B. (1996). *Learning as a Way of Being: Strategies for Survival in a World of Permanent White Water.* San Francisco: Jossey-Bass.

Wilson, J. P. (2005). *Human Resource Development: Learning and Training for Individuals and Organizations* (2nd ed.). London: Kogan Page.

ADDITIONAL RESOURCE

Vaill, P. B. (1989). *Managing as a Performing Art: New Ideas for a World of Chaotic Change.* San Francisco: Jossey-Bass.

Elizabeth Fuseler Avery

chapter 4

How to Set Goals

OALS ARE STATEMENTS THAT DESCRIBE WHAT YOUR ORGANI-
zation would like to accomplish. Barney and Griffin (1992)
state that organizational goals serve four basic functions:
they provide guidance and direction, facilitate planning,
motivate and inspire employees, and help organizations
evaluate and control performance. Goals can set a course
of action for staff and give rationale for decision making on
how staff development is presented, funded, and assessed. With the fast pace of
change in libraries, although goals are the ends toward which your efforts will
be directed, they may need to be changed from year to year or more frequently.

Setting goals for staff development is part of a process of continuous
improvement for the organization and the individuals who make up the organization. As in *kaizen*, a Japanese management philosophy, there is a "need
to be constantly on the lookout for new and better ways to accomplish things
through gradual, unending improvements" (Rohlander, 1999, pp. 10–11). Even
though goal setting for staff development is time and energy intensive, goals
provide a map for controlled passage through a chaotic state from a current,
real-time situation to a refocused, more desirable situation. If the organization
asks staff members to make changes in their behaviors and methods of work,
it is critical for the goal setters "to find ways to create a line of sight between

employees and the organization's critical success measure" (Ray & Altmansberger, 1999, p. 41). To assist in the design of goals for a planned system of change that enhances the services of the organization and supports the adaptation of the persons involved, the questions that follow in this chapter can serve as signposts through the chaos.

Goals must be established in a well-defined context; if not, they are meaningless. Among the factors of a well-defined context are the following:

- The reality factor—goals must work from the current reality.
- The plausibility—possibility factor—goals must be capable of being achieved.
- The openness factor—both the goal orientation and the goal content must be known.

Goals, Objectives, Benchmarking

Goals and objectives are directly related to one another, but they are not the same. A goal is a statement—a large, overarching statement that describes what you want to accomplish. Goals aren't easily measured.

Objectives are specific, measurable action statements that describe specific things to be accomplished to reach the goal. Objectives are usually constructed using a measurable verb, they establish criteria, and they set conditions. They form the basis for the activities in your staff development plan.

Benchmarking can be used in two ways. One, the institutional benchmark, is the ongoing, systematic process for measuring and comparing one institution's practices with others that have been determined to exhibit best practices. It can be used to help an institution discover how it can improve its processes or services. Using this benchmark, gaps in the institution's staff development program can be identified. When using institutional benchmarking, it is essential that the peer group be closely aligned in size and mission to your institution.

The second, the individual benchmark, identifies the knowledge, skills, and abilities necessary to achieve superior performance. Using this benchmark set allows you to identify needs for training. When using individual benchmarking, it should be clear whether the knowledge, skills, and abilities pertain to all members in specific job classification, all members of the organization, or to a specific individual.

There have been two schools of thought on how to set goals for a library-wide program, either top down or bottom up. The traditional theories of motivation, such as goal-setting theory, present goals as something that are given to individuals, are accepted, and the individuals are motivated by the reward they will get for achieving the goal set for them (Parker, Bindl, & Strauss, 2010). However, individuals want to take more control of their professional development. Newer generations realize the need for continuous training and want to be involved (Lancaster & Stillman, 2002).

Writing Clear and Achievable Goals and Objectives

GETTING STARTED

- Who should be involved in setting staff development goals?
- Should everyone in the organization be involved, or should there be representatives from each department or area? Should outside consultants and the training officer be involved?
- Who will review the goals and set priorities?
- Will the director, the personnel officer, administrative group, or a staff development committee be able to provide the big picture and put the goals in the larger organizational context?
- What is the purpose of the staff development program?
- Is the staff development program for job orientation, job skills enhancement or training, professional development to cultivate or extend current knowledge and abilities, or innovative or change-making training?
- Where and when will the group meet?
- Which will be more effective—a retreat out of the building or regularly scheduled meetings?
- Does where, when, and how often group members meet affect the quality of the goals?
- How much time should be spent on goal planning?
- Can too much time be spent on goal planning, sacrificing staff development time?
- Will a timeline facilitate a timely completion of goal setting?

THE LARGER VIEW

- What is the organization's mission or vision statement?
- Does each department in the organization have its own mission or vision statement?
- Do individual staff members have mission or vision statements?
- What are the implications of future library trends and challenges?
- How does the current reality support achieving the goals?
- What is possible based on the financial situation?
- What is possible based on the time frame?
- What is possible based on current staffing patterns?
- What is possible based on current staff skills and knowledge?
- What is possible based on current technology?
- What is possible based on organizational culture?
- What is the desired change that the goals should target?
- Is the desired change realistic for the organization?
- Is the desired change possible based on current reality?
- Will the desired change improve or enhance the organization?
- What are the consequences of not setting coherent goals?

THE DETAILS

- What is the foundation on which staff development goals will be built?
- How can widespread support for the goals be obtained?
- What channels of communication are in place to communicate goals?
- What methods will be employed to reach agreement or consensus on the goals?
- What written form will the staff development goals take?
- Who will decide the format?
- How often will the form be revised to reflect altered situations?
- What processes must be put in motion to begin movement toward the goals?
- What training is necessary to reach the goals?
- Who will provide the training?
- Is the training affordable?
- Will the training be onetime or ongoing?

- What long-term, intermediate, and short-term objectives are markers to show that the process is moving toward established goals?
- What does successfully achieving the goal look like?
- How will achievement of the goals be evaluated?
- Who will conduct the evaluations?
- Will the evaluations be ongoing after the initial training to determine whether the goals were the appropriate change for the organization?
- How will the evaluation results be applied to staff work?

WHAT TO CONSIDER

- The chaotic consideration involves the recognition that staff development not only consists of acquiring new skills but also requires behavior and attitude changes that may be difficult and uncomfortable until they are embedded.
- The circular consideration includes the recognition that setting goals for staff development never ceases; there must be circular thinking in the sense of continually establishing new goals and adapting existing goals.
- The cumulation consideration pertains to the recognition that gains must occur as the process proceeds; that the gains are changes that must build on prior learning and have a supportive base in the organization.
- The culmination consideration incorporates the recognition that there may be intermittent pauses, planned or spontaneous, in the staff development process that may be used to observe accomplishments vis-à-vis staff growth and learning, the recognition that a sequence of these pauses can culminate in successful change and accomplishment of goals.

WHAT TO EVALUATE

- How will the accomplishment of the goals affect the staff morale, knowledge, and performance? Are the goals relevant enough to increase the skills and effectiveness of staff members? Will reaching the goals give individual staff members greater satisfaction and opportunity for growth (Kiewitt, 1992)?

- Do the goals focus on desired outputs rather than inputs?
- Do the goals address the issues that need to be addressed? "There is little to be gained from an activity that explores group problem solving if this is not an issue that needs to be addressed" (Rylatt & Lohan, 1997, p. 249).
- Are they specific, not vague? Do they avoid using jargon?
- Are they consistent with one another? For example, you can't give advanced PowerPoint training before the introductory class.
- What are the consequences of not reaching the goal? Will other goals or evaluations be affected?
- Will achievement of some goals be rewarded with special recognition or merit increase (Kiewitt, 1992)?
- Are the goals flexible? Is there a way to change or add programs to meet newly identified needs? Can they change with organizational changes?

Assessment

Assessment is essential to know whether you have reached you goal. Assessment can also be used as feedback to start another cycle of goal setting and moving the organization forward.

An established acronym, SMART, can help you create objectives for the goals that are easily assessed (Doran, 1981). Although there are some different interpretations of the acronym, in general SMART stands for the following:

Specific: The assessment answers the six *W* questions: who, what, where, when, which, and why.

Measurable: Is there a metric you can use to measure the success of individual programs and the overall program?

Achievable: If the objectives support long-range goals, are the current goals planned in logical stages to lead up to the long-range goals (Kiewitt, 1992)?

Realistic (or relevant): Can you accomplish the goals in the given time frame? Are there too many concurrent goals and objectives? Although

the goals should be challenging, they must be realistic for the staff to
support them.

Time based: Specific time limits or deadlines are established for achieving the goal.

Sometimes the acronym is expanded to SMARTER, where E stands for "evaluate" and R for "reevaluate."

Every objective does not have to have all five criteria. However, the more
of the criteria that are in your objective, the easier and better the assessment of
your program will be.

Conclusion

Supervisors and managers serve an important function in assisting individual
staff members in fitting their personal and professional goals into those of the
organization so that ongoing improvements occur. For this to happen, the goals
must be believable, clearly defined, and based in current reality. When the goals
are acceptable and desired by the individuals and the organization, they can be
visualized and achieved.

REFERENCES

Barney, J. B., & Griffin, R. W. (1992). *The Management of Organizations*. Boston, MA:
Houghton Mifflin.

Doran, G. T. (1981). "There's a S.M.A.R.T. Way to Write Management's Goals and Objectives." *Management Review, 70*(11), 35–36.

Kiewitt, E. L. (1992). "How to Set Goals." In A. Grodzins Lipow, & D. A. Carver (Eds.),
Staff Development: A Practical Guide (2nd ed., pp. 554–556). Chicago, IL:
American Library Association.

Lancaster, L. C., & Stillman, D. C. (2002). *When Generations Collide: Who They Are.
Why They Clash. How to Solve the Generational Puzzle at Work*. New York:
HarperCollins.

Parker, S. K., Bindl, U. K., & Strauss, K. (2010). "Making Things Happen: A Model of
Proactive Motivation." *Journal of Management, 36*(4), 827–856.

Ray, H. H., & Altmansberger, H. N. (1999). "Going for the Gold: Introducing Goalshar-
ing in a Public Sector Organization." *Compensation and Benefits Review, 31*(3),
40–45.

Rohlander, D. G. (1999). "How to Achieve Personal and Organizational Goals in 1999." *Financial Services Advisor, 142*(1), 10–11.

Rylatt, A., & Lohan, K. (1997). *Creating Training Miracles.* San Francisco: Pfeiffer.

ADDITIONAL RESOURCE

Baker, D. (2004, April 1). *Writing Objectives: Rationale and Strategies.* Presentation at the Monthly Medical Education Discussion Session, College of Medicine, Florida State University, Tallahassee. Retrieved from www.docstoc.com/docs/44518979/Writing-Objectives

Julia Blixrud

chapter 5

Getting Started

Questions to Ask

TAKING THE FIRST STEP TO DEVELOP A STAFF DEVELOPMENT PRO-gram can appear daunting, but there are ways to approach the process that can make it less overwhelming. Steps taken in project- and program-planning activities will help even the novice developer create an engaging and desired set of learning experiences to meet the needs of library staff. In most organizations, individuals from any level can take the initiative to plan and execute some sort of staff development activity, and they are encouraged to do so. A single enthusiastic individual can generate enough initial interest from staff members to participate in single programs and ultimately a full curriculum. Subsequent activities then may lend themselves to the work of a task force or committee.

Typical project and program planning includes stages in which an articulation of the program's overall objectives is made, beneficiaries are identified, time frames and resource needs are specified, and success criteria are established. The most important element is to create a clear set of objectives for what you want to accomplish. Subsequent steps in the planning process will address those objectives, so the more focused your objectives, the more likely you are to be successful. This process is best used for smaller, targeted events.

A detailed planning process can be conducted by following the program development model from the University of Wisconsin Extension (2003) that includes situational analysis, priority setting, program action (the logic model), and evaluation. The process can be applied to single events but is better suited to multiyear programs. This model, though seemingly complex, can focus attention on all elements needed in developing a full staff development program. The situational analysis is a needs analysis set in the context of an organization. It provides a means for individuals to express their preferences and helps build support for the program. Setting priorities requires an understanding of the mission of the institution or unit and the resources available to meet the overall goals of the program. The logic model provides a sequence of actions linking investments to results. Its components include inputs, outputs, outcomes, assumptions, and external factors. Finally, evaluation involves the gathering and analysis of data to improve subsequent activities.

Most colleges and universities (e.g., University of Pennsylvania, Division of Human Resources, 2007) have staff development programs in their human resources departments, and academic librarians would be wise to consult with them in the establishment of staff development programs. Similarly, school districts will have ongoing training and certification programs in which school librarians can build programs. City and county governments may have general technical or management programs that can be incorporated into public library staff development opportunities. And special librarians may find connections in the training or human resources departments of their parent corporations or organizations.

This chapter is intended to provide a general framework and some suggested questions that you might ask yourself as you plan your staff development activities. There are no absolutes, as institutions and individuals differ, but the questions are intended to be a guide for your initial thinking and consideration.

A First Step: Singular Events

One of the best ways to approach staff development is to plan a specific event. The idea for your event can come from your own experience or can be developed through conversation with colleagues. Having identified a potential area of interest by your library staff, you can arrange an event about something that has appeal to several individuals. Taking this on as a project will ensure that you address all the details. Here are some of the questions to ask yourself:

What is the precise topic for this event?
- Can it be expressed clearly?
- What is the evidence of interest in or need for it?

What is the intended outcome for this event?
- Is the event to help staff develop new skills?
- Is the event introducing staff to new technologies?
- Is the event being planned to increase knowledge about a particular topic with which staff is unfamiliar?
- Is the event intended to change perspectives or behaviors about a specific issue?

How will you measure the benefits for this program?
- Can you document improved performance?
- Will you provide a means to evaluate increased new knowledge?

Who is the audience for this event?
- Is the event focused on one department or unit or the whole library?
- Is all staff expected to attend this event or is attendance optional?
- Will staff be invited or appointed to attend?
- What is the maximum attendance for your site? The minimum to hold the event?
- Could we invite staff from outside the library? From other libraries in the area?

Who else should be involved in planning for this event?
- Will you be calling for volunteers and accepting everyone who offers to help?
- Do you have a particular set of skills needed to organize this event?
- Is there a mechanism to identify individuals on the basis of their skill (e.g., technical, communication, organizational contacts)?

What kind of administrative support is needed for the event?
- Must all events be approved prior to their being offered?
- What is the process for obtaining support?
- Can you articulate benefits for the event to the administration to engender their support?
- Will administrative support be useful in encouraging attendance?

What is the best format for delivery of this event?

Formal
- Should this be a workshop with a staff or external leader(s)?
- Is the topic best presented as a seminar with invited speakers?
- Would a webcast (either in real time or prerecorded) followed by facilitated staff discussion be the best approach?

Informal
- Can you gather staff together for a brown-bag lunch or afternoon coffee?
- Would a prerecorded podcast that individuals review at their desks work well in your environment?
- Could you share the information through an e-mail exchange or a wiki?

What kind of facilities and equipment are needed for the event?
- How large a room is needed?
- How should the room be arranged (e.g., computer lab, lecture, small-group discussion, viewing a video)?
- Can the light and temperature be adjusted?
- What kind of technology is needed (e.g., computer, screen, microphone)?
- Does the room have enough electrical outlets?
- Is wireless Internet available?
- What software is needed?
- What other materials are needed (e.g., notepads, flip charts, markers)?
- Will food be served?
- Will there be a break, and are there restroom facilities nearby?

What resources are needed to support this event?

- How much time will it take to prepare for the event?
- What advance notice is needed for invitations to the event (careful thought to scheduling will reduce potential conflicts and maximize attendance)?
- Are external speakers being contacted?
- Does this event require use of a room that needs to be scheduled?
- Do handouts need to be prepared and duplicated?
- Is preenrollment required?
- Does someone need to be in charge of audiovisual equipment?
- What kind of setup needs to be done for the room on the day of the event?
- How will refreshments be handled?
- Who will prepare name tags, registration materials, and evaluations?

How should you publicize your event?

- Does the description accurately reflect the goals of the event and the intended audience?
- Where can you distribute information about the event (e.g., flyers, staff bulletin board, e-mail distribution lists, note from administrator)?

How should the event be evaluated?

- What evaluation tools will you use to measure the outcome of the event?
- Will you consider repeating the event?
- What went well with the event?
- What did you learn from planning this event that can be applied to future events?

Will there be follow-up to the event?

- Will there be reinforcement of learning from the event?
- What additional potential topics were raised as a result of this event?

Many libraries have held single staff development events, and you may find it beneficial to talk with someone who has held an event similar to one you are planning. An online search may identify institutions or individuals who are willing to share some of their experience. A common topic is training for new system enhancements that you might arrange in consultation with a vendor. Communication with other libraries that use the same system could allow use of a preexisting outline. Another single event might be to introduce staff to an unfamiliar national issue, such as orphan works legislation or access to federally funded research.

Building Interest: Thematic Topics

Upon completion of a singular event, an evaluation of it may yield additional ideas for other topics. These events could be conducted in a similar manner to the first step (i.e., organizing a singular event), but setting them up as a series of related topics held over the course of a period of months or perhaps a year will result in additional benefits. Library staff will become accustomed to these kinds of opportunities for staff development and will offer additional suggestions for topics. In addition, other individuals may surface who are interested in helping put together a specific event but may not want to be involved in staff development activities on a continual basis.

Some thematic topics that could be of interest include the changing nature of scholarly communication, the use of new technologies for reference services, assessment tools for improved library performance, intellectual freedom, information fluency, and working with different types of clientele. Each of these could be developed into several events with a unifying theme. The questions to ask for each event would be the same as those asked for a first step, but the overall objective and subsequent evaluation will focus on the knowledge gained throughout the series.

As an example, under the auspices of the Association of Research Libraries and the Association of College and Research Libraries' Institute on Scholarly Communication, a guide to program planning was developed to help institutions create ongoing programs addressing the complex issues of scholarly communication (Fowler, Persily, & Stemper, 2011).

A Formula for Success: Sequenced Events

The positive movement from singular events through a set of thematic topics may propel you into the development of a series of events and, subsequently, a formal program. As that program arises, there are new questions you need to ask in your library:

What is considered staff development in the context of our organization?
- Do we have common definitions for training, professional development, and other important terms?
- How will our program support our organizational mission?
- What is the relationship between program support from the perspective of the institution and that of the individual?

Who is the staff development program designed for?
- Will individual staff be required to participate in all parts of the program, or will parts be voluntary?
- What will the expectations be of supervisors for support of staff training?

What structure will sustain the formal program?
- How will we develop a formal policy for our program?
- Is administration supportive of a staff development program?
- What are the expected outcomes of our program?
- Are there priorities among types of events or participating staff members?
- Will ad hoc individuals or an appointed committee or task force do the planning and preparation for events?

What resources are available for the program?
- If funds are available, how will they be allocated?
- Who will approve allocation of funds?
- How will trainers and speakers be identified?

What types of events will achieve the goals of the program?
- What is the focus of the program (e.g., skills, behavior changes, new knowledge)?

- How will evaluation be conducted?
- Will there be follow-up for individual program events?
- How will ideas for new program elements be solicited?

Maintaining the Momentum: A Continuing Program

Any staff development program should be designed to support the library's mission, vision, and strategic goals. It should also provide opportunities for staff education, training, and career development that would help them meet their own personal goals. In addition, the best programs offer training that creates opportunities for flexible staffing options. Begin to develop your ideas for a staff development program by reviewing those at other libraries. A search of the literature and websites (and use of this guide) will provide useful information to create a program that is meaningful to you and your staff. The University Libraries at University of Maryland, College Park, has developed a comprehensive staff development program. The program supports both individual and organizational learning, and the Learning Curriculum gives staff a plan for their own skill development (University of Maryland, University Libraries, 2008).

Gathering information routinely and systematically on current staff skills and interests is an important part of program maintenance. Even the best program requires continual evaluation to make sure it meets the needs of your staff. Once training and development needs of staff are determined, it is easier to create a program that is aligned both with staff needs and with the library's strategic priorities. It is important to systematically review the program's outcomes. Each program component should have specific and measureable objectives by which you can demonstrate your success.

Once established, the staff development program cannot be static. There will be times when training is required to address an immediate need, such as a system change. In other cases, programs might be needed to support general professional development or conducted to help raise awareness of new and emerging issues affecting your library. A comprehensive staff development program is also beneficial to establish a common base of understanding for library staff and ensures the use of a common language for discussion. Shared experiences help to improve communication and cooperation.

Also be aware that in developing programs, learning styles differ. Offer different modes of delivery so that the needs of most people can be met. If education is one of the core missions of the library, then libraries need to make the same commitment to educating their staff as they do to their users. Staff development programs help staff become better skilled and enhance their own personal development. All it takes is a systematic plan to provide opportunities for all, and that can be done just by taking the first step.

EXAMPLES OF STAFF DEVELOPMENT PROGRAM CONTENT

Enhance technical skills or retrain
- Use of new hardware and software for library functions
- New data-entry procedures
- Web 2.0 (e.g., blogs, wikis, social networking)
- Job rotation
- Writing grant proposals
- Digitization techniques

Personal performance
- Time management
- Writing (e.g., reports, correspondence, professional literature)
- Self-motivation
- Effective presentation skills
- Communication skills
- Working in groups
- Balancing life and work
- Project management
- Customer service

Management
- Planning and conducting meetings
- Job redesign
- Team leaders
- Supervision
- Decision making
- Performance evaluation
- Use of statistics
- Team building
- Space reallocation
- Handling change

- Diversity
- Americans with Disabilities Act
- Training new employees
- Managing students and temporary workers
- Dealing with difficult patrons
- Coaching skills
- Organizational assessment

Understanding of current issues
- Copyright and intellectual property
- Author rights
- Changing workforce
- Generational learners
- Diversity
- Library funding
- Scholarly communication
- Preserving digital objects

REFERENCES

Fowler, K., Persily, G., & Stemper, J. (2011). "Developing a Scholarly Communication Program in Your Library." Retrieved from www.arl.org/sc/institute/fair/scprog/index.shtml

University of Maryland, University Libraries. (2008). "The Learning Organization." Retrieved from www.lib.umd.edu/groups/learning/learning.org.html

University of Pennsylvania, Division of Human Resources. (2007). "Performance and Staff Development Program." Retrieved from www.hr.upenn.edu/StaffRelations/Performance

University of Wisconsin Extension. (2003). "Program Development and Evaluation." Retrieved from www.uwex.edu/ces/pdande/progdev/index.html

ADDITIONAL RESOURCES

American Management Association, www.amanet.org

American Society for Training and Development, www.astd.org

Barbazette, J. (2006). *Training Needs Assessment: Methods, Tools, and Techniques.* San Francisco: Pfeiffer.

Barbazette, J. (2008). *Managing the Training Function for Bottom-Line Results: Tools, Models, and Best Practices.* San Francisco: Pfeiffer.

Biech, E. (Ed.). (2008). *ASTD Handbook for Workplace Learning Professionals.* Alexandria, VA: ASTD Press.

Learning Round Table, http://alalearning.org

Noe, R. A. (2010). *Employee Training and Development* (5th ed.). New York, NY: McGraw-Hill.

Russell, K., Ames-Oliver, K., Fund, L., Proctor, T., & Vannaman, M. (2003). "Organizational Development, Best Practices, and Employee Development." *Library Administration and Management, 17,* 189–195.

Part II

Developing Your Staff

Carol A. Kochan and Sandra J. Weingart

chapter 6 / # Developing Orientation Programs for New Employees

ESTABLISHING AN EFFECTIVE EMPLOYEE ORIENTATION PRO-gram is an important part of the training and retention of new workers. It is a chance for supervisors to communicate policies and performance standards and to begin the training that will help establish a successful career. Too often, new employee orientation is conducted haphazardly, with few goals communicated to the new hire. Such situations can be prevented easily, as an orientation program is simple to administer once a master plan has been developed. This chapter presents ideas for developing an efficient and effective program for bringing new employees into your library and getting them off to a good start.

Before the First Day

You've selected the best candidate for your job position, and now you need to focus on ensuring that she is well trained and able to learn the necessary job tasks and customer service skills effectively. After the time you've invested in selecting the right candidate, you'll want to ensure that you can retain her in your organization. Before the new hire arrives, outline the skills and training needed to perform the job well. Stay in touch with the new employee to answer any questions and provide her with additional information about the job. A schedule of the first day and week and a checklist of training activities must be developed in advance, with any appointments confirmed. Be sure that the new employee's workstation is ready before she arrives. Computers should be loaded with both the software needed to do the job and any orientation materials. Make sure old files have been cleared off and that the computer monitor and keyboard are clean. Work spaces should be tidy, necessary files organized, and the space free of the detritus of previous occupants.

Communicating with your new employee before the first day of work provides many opportunities. This is a time to create a good first impression in this new relationship and to make sure that your employee is prepared for the first day on the job. You can help him acclimate in a new community if a move is involved and reassure him that you are looking forward to having him on board in your organization. Starting a new job can be an exciting but difficult time, requiring both adjustment and preparation. As an employer you can help make this transition period easier by providing any information he needs and offering assistance getting settled in the new community. Although some of the suggestions here apply specifically to professional librarians, many can be adapted to other positions in the library. Regardless of the type of job and whether the employee is a local hire or is from another city and relocating to your area, the basic message of welcome and assistance in the transition applies to every new employee.

Information about the job is always useful to new employees. Although you covered the general job description during the interview process, providing more details about the job, coworkers, and supervisor(s) is always welcome. Sending a detailed outline of beginning projects, a schedule of meetings for the first week, an outline of needed training, as well as providing the employee with her new e-mail address and telephone number, an indication of dress codes (so she doesn't have to guess what to wear on the first day), and so on, will be appreciated. A call to the new employee the day before the first day of work is a good time to answer any last-minute questions and remind him where his office is located in the library. If possible, complete human resources paperwork and forward any relevant institutional information in advance, so that employees don't spend their first day at work filling out personnel papers and reading manuals, which can squelch even the most enthusiastic recruit's desire to show up for the second day of work. Make sure that employees are aware of your institution's payroll schedule. That first paycheck may be a long time coming, especially for student workers.

If your employee is relocating for the new job, she will welcome information about the community. Information about housing, child care, local schools, transportation options (including parking at the worksite and tips on how to avoid commuter traffic jams, as well as public transportation options), cultural resources, and other details about the community can help smooth the transition. You might add maps, directories, and links to the website of the local newspaper to this list.

First Day

The day has finally come; your new hire will be here any minute. As supervisor, it is your responsibility to welcome the new hire and get him off to a good start. Greet him as he arrives on the first day. Any other staff members participating in the orientation process should be on hand as well. Present your new hire with a written schedule of training events and participants. We have found it useful to include a checklist of tasks and policies the newcomer will master. Both you and he should initial items as they are completed. A good schedule includes time for assimilation, reflection, and questions. Although there will be common elements for all new hires, each schedule should be customized to allow for individual learning styles and speed. Discuss expectations, both yours and his. Many of us have at some time experienced the frustration of being willing to do what was wanted, if only somebody would tell us what it was. Don't subject your new hires to this uncertainty.

After your initial discussion, it's time to tour your facility and introduce your newcomer to new colleagues. The new hire needs to learn the general functions and personnel of each department so that she knows what happens where and who does it. This will help her begin to establish her mental model of the organization and her place in it. Also, if she will be working at a public service desk, she may need to direct patrons at some point. End the tour at her work space. Whether it is a desk in an open-plan office, a cubicle, or a private office, her name should be on it. Show her where to find supplies and the locations of essentials such as the break room and lavatory. Check to make sure that the appropriate human resources documentation is complete and that your new hire has been introduced to institutional policies regarding leave, scheduling, and performance reviews. Review the activities of the department and her specific responsibilities in them. Be sure to include an overview of the library website, including the mission statement and those features most relevant to her responsibilities. Classified employees and student workers usually begin their practical training here, most often under the guidance of a more experienced coworker.

A critical component of an individual's success in an organization is his integration into its social structure. Friendly invitations from coworkers to share a break or a meal together indicate that they welcome his presence and want him to thrive. A recent new hire in our department commented that such invitations were the thing that truly made her feel like she had made the right decision in accepting her position.

First Week

The first day at a new job provides a deluge of information that your employee needs time to process and assimilate. In the first week, she should be ready to delve more deeply into her job duties and begin to gain an understanding about her role in the organization. For all levels of employees, training for specific tasks begins here under the guidance of either their direct supervisor or a more experienced coworker. Shadowing is often an effective method to accomplish this purpose, as it allows newcomers to participate in the task as soon as they are ready. Remember that she will be eager to demonstrate her abilities; therefore, structure the training period so that the new employee is accomplishing real work as soon as possible. It's utterly disheartening to spend the first several weeks of a new job slogging through manuals and trying to figure out what to do.

Provide documentation of which tasks will be expected, the detailed procedures for performing them, the time frame in which they are to be performed, and the workflow for the department. Be sure to indicate which tasks have priority for the department. Begin with the most critical tasks to be learned. In addition, setting a tone for positive customer service interactions is vital. You need to model appropriate methods of customer service protocol and demonstrate when patrons should be referred to other departments. You'll also want to review her role statement at the professional level and the job performance standards document at the paraprofessional level, so your employee is aware how her work will be evaluated.

At the professional level, each employee should meet with department heads and other key personnel to gain an overview of the ways in which the component units work together to accomplish the mission of the organization. This is a good time for you to go over the library's strategic goals, so your new hire is able to comprehend the library's vision and understand what components and projects he should focus on.

Every employee, whatever the position, should know what actions to take in a variety of emergency situations. Specific responsibilities and chain of command must be delineated to ensure the safety of patrons and staff and to protect the collections. This information should be available on the library website. You should also point out the fire extinguishers and emergency exits nearest to her work area. Many workplaces are also establishing an emergency communication network, so that students and staff are notified in the event of a crisis; you'll want to make sure that your new hire is signed up for that service.

Check in with your newcomer from time to time during this week. Find out how things are going and adapt the schedule as needed. Some will seek new challenges and ask questions readily; others will need more encouragement to achieve their potential. This initial period will have a great impact on whether your new employee stays with the organization and thrives or seek opportunities elsewhere, so make sure that you're providing him with the information he needs to be successful in his job role.

Continuing Training

It is important to follow up with your new hire to ensure that she understands all the aspects of her new job. She had an enormous amount of information to process and assimilate during her first week. In the rush to get up to speed, it is easy for small but critical pieces of information to be lost or overlooked. Make yourself available to your new hire for consultation on those questions that arise as she becomes more familiar with her job and the institution. There always seem to be exceptions to policies or procedures that pop up unexpectedly. Review her work and provide thoughtful feedback. This should include praise for material mastered as well as correction in those areas that require it.

Student workers often perform the most basic tasks, but they are often also the first people to interact with patrons. Take the time to be sure that they understand the details of their jobs. Once they have mastered them, provide cross-training for other activities in the department. This provides them greater variety in their daily routines and allows for greater flexibility in covering essential operations when coworkers are out.

Cross-training opportunities should be provided for classified employees as well. Being capable of and comfortable with performing the duties of other positions in the department makes employees more valuable to the library and more confident in their own abilities. Keep an eye out for training opportunities in both library skills and other career enhancement areas and identify which will be most useful for which individuals.

Professional librarians should meet with key colleagues in other departments to become familiar with local collections. Reference personnel should meet with fellow subject specialists for training in relevant resources available in your library. Assignments that occur regularly and with large numbers of students should be emphasized as well. Our university has one such assignment in landscape architecture that requires very specific tools and has a very tight time frame. It is much easier for newcomers if an experienced hand shows them how to deal with it. If your new hire is on the tenure track, provide the relevant sections of the university code and any guidelines on preparing a portfolio. Inform her of the composition of her promotion and tenure committee and whether each candidate has a separate committee or there is one that reviews all candidates in a given year.

Librarianship is evolving and changing at an increasingly rapid pace and continuing training is necessary for all employees. After the initial period of employment, this is no longer orientation to the profession or the individual library and falls under the heading of ongoing staff development, which is covered elsewhere in this handbook.

Conclusion

Preparing a new employee orientation program takes some time and planning. Each position must be analyzed to determine the skills necessary for the successful completion of it. It is also important to encourage positive staff interactions, which will assist newcomers in becoming familiar with the overall operation of the library and in forming collegial relationships. The end result is an appropriately prepared employee who is readily able to assimilate work policies and to perform at a proficient level. Once an initial orientation program has been established, it is relatively simple to adapt it for all new employees.

Joan Giesecke and Beth McNeil

chapter 7

Core Competencies for Libraries and Library Staff

ORE COMPETENCIES DEFINE THE KNOWLEDGE, SKILLS, AND abilities that every employee needs for an organization to be successful. Core competencies become the foundation for staff development programs and for planning organizational improvements. Identification of competencies is crucial in today's changing environment because competencies "essentially reframe work by deconstructing positions or jobs and rephrasing their content as components or values" (Soutter, 2007, p. 2).

The concept of core competencies has been well explored in the business literature (Giesecke & McNeil, 1999) and a simple Google search in November 2011 for the term *core competencies* yielded more than 5.8 million sites. A similar search of Library Science and Technology Abstracts yielded 271 articles between 1990 and 2011.

For libraries, several articles describe lists of competencies based on surveys of library directors and others working in the field, in relation to library school curriculum. Woodsworth and Lester (1991) address the competencies necessary for library school graduates by first examining the future of the research library and the staffing requirements that will be necessary. Beginning with the mission statement of the future research library, Woodsworth and Lester (1991) determine staff responsibilities and then define the necessary competencies. Woodsworth and Westermann (1995) discuss professional education for librarians, as well as continuing education needs, also based on the future research library model. They address necessary core and elective courses for library school students along with the integration of library science and information technology skills. The authors emphasize the need to consider the shared goals of both groups: helping library users with all aspects of information management. Surveys of library school alumni offer suggestions for restructuring library school curriculum in an article by Buttlar and Du Mont (1996). The alumni emphasize educating students to fit into the culture of the organization, regardless of the position they may fill. Competencies are listed by type of library and vary by level of experience. Other articles that focus on competencies for librarians working in specific areas or types of libraries, such as reference librarians in an academic library or a special library, also include lists of specialized competencies (Ojala, 1993; Rockman, Massey-Burzio, & Ritch, 1991; Stafford & Serban, 1990). A recurring theme in these articles is the "need for risk takers and synthesizers with the ability to function in an atmosphere of ambiguity and change" (Woodsworth & Westermann, 1995, p. 53).

In a review of articles on academic library competencies, Soutter (2007) describes the wide range of materials appearing between 2001 and 2005 in the library literature. She noted that management-related articles were a primary focus of thirty-five of the sixty-six articles she reviewed. McNeil (2002) reports on core competencies in academic research libraries in a 2002 ARL SPEC Kit survey. During this same time period, the American Library Association (*ALA's Core Competences*, 2008) explored core competencies for librarians and developed a list of competencies for all graduates of ALA-accredited master's programs. Divisions in the ALA and special library organizations have also developed competencies for librarians in specialized areas, including medical librarianship, school librarianship, and special librarianship.

Houghton-Jan (2007) notes the progress made in developing lists of competencies for specializations in libraries and outlines technology competencies. She describes the importance of every member of the library staff having a solid foundation in and understanding of the technologies that are the core of the library or information world.

The temptation to outline an extensive list of the knowledge, skills, and traits that librarians and library staff need as found in some articles could derail an organization's efforts to identify and work with core competencies. As Penniman (1991) noted in *Journal of Academic Librarianship*, "As the seminal article in the *Harvard Business Review* by Prahalad and Hamel (1990) claims, successful organizations of the future will focus on a small number of fundamental competencies and will transcend fragmentation of these competencies by creating strategic architecture that serves as a road map for the future." (p. 211)

Competencies are more than just lists of admirable traits. They must be an integral part of all aspects of the library's strategic framework and be incorporated into all job descriptions and performance evaluations. Only when core competencies are fully integrated into the library culture will the library be able to change and sustain those changes through turbulent times.

Developing Core Competencies: One Library's Experience

At the University of Nebraska–Lincoln (UNL) Libraries, librarians and staff understand the need to continually adapt to a changing environment. In 1996 the libraries began the process of becoming a learning organization, "an organization skilled at creating, acquiring, and transferring knowledge, and at modifying its behavior to reflect new knowledge and insights" (Giesecke & McNeil, 2004, p. 55). To be successful, learning organizations need to learn to incorporate new knowledge into the organization to improve services and workflow. Learning organizations are action oriented. Change has to occur for an organization to become a learning organization. All members of the library staff need to take an active interest in learning and in improving the organization. Staff needs to be engaged in the organization for the organization to improve. Staff can no longer sit back and wait for others to tell them what to do. They must take an active part in the workings of the organization.

The changing expectations for staff and the need to think beyond just task-related skills to more systems thinking led managers to understand that they needed to think in terms of hiring different kinds of employees: employees who are flexible and change oriented.

To help managers understand what type of staff were needed and to help staff understand the changing expectations, the libraries embarked on a process to identify core competencies for all staff.

A committee was formed to begin to develop a list of competencies. The committee included representatives of each of three employee groups: the office, service, or library assistant positions, the first-line supervisors or managers who are not library faculty, and the library faculty. The administration's charge to the committee was to develop core competencies for library staff and to give strong consideration to flexibility, information literacy, and adaptability to new technology.

The human resources department on campus was also included in the development process. Although not members of the committee, the managers from human resources needed to be involved as their staff handle the initial screening for job applicants for many of the open positions in the libraries. Human resources would need to know what competencies were necessary for library staff and how to determine whether applicants for office, service or managerial and professional positions met those competencies.

Committee members researched competencies in libraries and businesses by looking for books and articles on competency modeling as well as lists of competencies already in place in organizations. In addition, the committee met with individuals with experience in development and implementing competencies.

The committee learned that the University of Nebraska Medical Center's (UNMC) human resources department, working together with line managers and an outside consultant, had developed a list of core competencies for all UNMC staff. When the UNMC representative met with the UNL Libraries' committee, the UNMC committee was in the process of revising the original list of competencies and developing in-depth screening and interview questions related to the revised competencies.

Although the UNMC competencies were not specifically for libraries or library staff, the committee was able to build on the work done at UNMC. Competencies listed by UNMC were very similar to competencies reported necessary for library work by Robbins and Licona (1994), including "flexibility, lifetime learning; people skills; technological skills; business skills, including marketing, negotiation, and strategic planning; and valuing diversity" (p. 7).

After much discussion and review of the competencies of many other organizations, the committee recommended a list of competencies that all library staff must demonstrate, regardless of staff group or line. The twelve core competencies included the following:

1. Analytical skills, problem solving, and decision making
2. Communication skills

3. Creativity and innovation
4. Effective leadership
5. Expertise and technical knowledge
6. Flexibility and adaptability
7. Interpersonal and group skills
8. Organizational understanding and systems thinking
9. Ownership and accountability
10. Planning and organizational skills
11. User satisfaction
12. Value management

Also developed for each of the twelve core competencies was a short definition and several actions listed.

These core competencies applied to all library staff, although some aspects or actions of each of the competencies might not apply to every staff person. Many similarities can be found between the list of core competencies and the staffing characteristics that Woodsworth and Lester (1991) identified as necessary:

> Strong user orientation; expertise in analysis of user needs; understanding of and ability to conduct research; orientation to information processes and products (not library services in the traditional sense); a broad knowledge of information resources (that is not format or institution specific); competency in the design and implementation of information products and systems, including databases and user profiles; self-identification as an information linking agent and as an information manager; and group management and team-building abilities. (p. 53)

In addition, the core competencies developed for the UNL Libraries' staff were similar to the educational competencies that Woodsworth and Westermann (1995) identified as necessary for librarians in the research library of the future, "competencies that included not only knowledge, comprehension, and applications but also analysis, synthesis, and evaluation." The areas that Woodsworth and Westermann (1995) identified include total information environment and the interconnections within it; information-seeking and usage behavior of individuals; political and decision-making processes; development of a long-range strategic planning mentality, with planning considered a process, not a product; interpersonal and small-group dynamics; organizational psychology and behavior; marketing; economics of information; team effectiveness; community analysis; evaluation methodologies; statistical analysis; and research methods.

The committee forwarded the list of competencies to libraries' management group for comments. With just a few changes, the management group approved the competencies. Most of the suggestions were minor changes in wording. One exception to this, however, was in regard to computer or technical expertise. Information technology and systems staff felt that a greater emphasis needed to be placed on technical expertise and that those specifics needed to be included in the core competencies. With assistance from the computer operations director, appropriate wording was added to the core competencies document. At this point, the draft of the core competencies was shared with human resources staff for input regarding use as a screening tool for staff applicants. After the meeting with human resources staff, all library staff had the opportunity to comment on competencies before final approval or acceptance was granted. Staff groups discussed competencies in their regular meetings, the committee members led small-group sessions from the group that developed the competencies, and a general discussion took place at an all-staff meeting.

In 1997, the core competency list was formally accepted, and plans for use of the list were developed. The group process used in the libraries for developing the list of core competencies proved particularly useful in helping staff understand the rationale for the list and in understanding ways that core competencies can be used in the organization. Because an open process with librarywide discussion was used to develop the list, the library staff supported the core competencies list and helped design ways to use core competencies in the libraries programs.

Core Competencies in the Larger Organization

At the University of Nebraska, the university addressed the need for core competencies shortly after the libraries developed the list of competencies for library staff. The human resources department started with the libraries' core competency list and broadened the language so that the concepts applied to all office service and managerial professional positions on campus. The university list includes eight competencies: accountability, adaptability, communication, customer or quality focus, inclusiveness, occupational knowledge or technical orientation, team focus, and leadership. The libraries worked with human resources to revise the library list from twelve to nine competencies, using the eight from the university and retaining the competency of problem solving and decision making. The libraries incorporated the definitions from human resources into the libraries' documents. By working with the university's human resources department, the libraries were successful in shaping a set of competencies that fit with the libraries' changing environment and reflected campus values and needs. Once competencies are developed, they can be used for recruiting, interviewing, staff development, and performance evaluation, for staff at all levels.

Implementing Core Competencies

The libraries began the implementation of the core competencies with a number of staff development programs. Shaughnessy (1992) discusses the importance of staff development programs in his article on developing competencies in research libraries. Staff at all levels must agree that some education or training are necessary to adapt to the changing future and to achieve the core competencies. At the UNL Libraries, staff development training in core competencies continues to be an integral part of the overall staff development program more than ten years after initial implementation. Training has included workshops on the core competencies, training for supervisors on how to interpret core competencies, and sessions with university human resources staff on the university's efforts to incorporate core competencies. The Staff Development Unit has also conducted training programs on specific competencies, including improving communication skills, diversity and inclusiveness, teamwork, and leadership. In addition, the technology department holds regular training sessions on new software packages and major upgrades so that all staff can stay current with the changing technologies in the libraries.

Incorporating core competencies into the recruitment process is another obvious implementation step to ensure that new members of the library staff have the needed knowledge, skills, and attributes, and demonstrate the ability, aptitude, and willingness, to continue to grow and develop.

Interview questions can help determine applicants' competencies: the skills, knowledge, and behaviors that make the applicant an acceptable candidate for a position. It was necessary to review the kinds of questions asked in interviews to ensure that the libraries recruit people who can perform a task well and who can work effectively in the organization in a time of change. A set of possible questions was developed for each competency and was shared with supervisors and search committees. No search committee or supervisor is expected to ask a job candidate every question. Before the interview, the supervisors and search committees decide which questions are most pertinent for the open position. Some questions apply to more than one competency and may be included in the list of interview questions in more than one area. Examples of three iterations of core competencies interview questions are included in Appendix A.

Performance Evaluations

The next phase of the process of integrating core competences into the operations of the library was to incorporate the core competency concepts into the performance evaluations. The libraries used a two-year phase-in approach to change the evaluation system. In the first year, 2005, the core competencies were reviewed with each employee at the time of his or her evaluation. Supervisors and employees discussed how the employee could meet the core competency and how the supervisor would measure the person's success in each area. This first year allowed staff to become familiar with the concepts and to test how best to demonstrate their skills. In the second year, the evaluation form was revised so that supervisors could evaluate employees on each of the competencies. The definitions of the competencies were included on the form to ensure that supervisors and employees were interpreting the concepts in the same way. After two years the libraries found that some supervisors were not taking the competencies into account in the overall rating for the employee. To help supervisors and employees recognize the importance of the competencies, the libraries, with the approval of human resources, determined that competencies would count for 50 percent of a person's rating. This way, supervisors could not as easily excuse behaviors that were not in line with the competencies. It also signaled to employees that the administration and the university were serious about the competencies and expected staff to meet these softer skills as well as the technical skills of their positions.

By 2008 the libraries found that supervisors were rewarding appropriate behaviors and were identifying problems that could then be addressed through the human resources system with appropriate documentation. The change in organizational climate as a result of the change in the reward system has been extremely positive. The few employees who could be called "toxic" found they no longer had the support of their colleagues. Some chose to leave, and others chose to change their behaviors to reflect the agreed-to standards in the library.

At Nebraska, staff development programs continue to reinforce the importance of the core competencies, and staff members are asking for more training in meeting the expectations in the competency. Behavior is following rewards and reinforcing a positive professional environment for everyone in the libraries.

The library faculty has taken a slightly different approach to the core competencies and performance evaluations. They chose to review and revise the libraries' promotion and tenure documents and to post tenure review documents to reflect the core competencies, relabeled as "organizational values and interpersonal skills." The faculty then included the organizational values in the written annual evaluation form, where they are considered of equal value with teaching, research, and service. The incorporation of behavioral guidelines in the faculty documents has provided the faculty with a way to sustain a conversation on overall climate and the impact of individual behaviors and skills on the overall effectiveness of the libraries.

Lessons Learned

A number of lessons were learned in the process of creating core competencies for the organization. Successful development and implementation of core competencies included the following:

> An open and inclusive process involving library faculty and staff in the development of the core competencies is crucial.
>
> Working closely with the institution's human resources department allowed the libraries to develop a set of competencies that addressed the libraries' needs and reflected the values of the larger organization.
>
> Staff development is a key factor in creating a successful change program. The organization has a responsibility to ensure that its employees have the resources and skills needed to perform the tasks in their positions.

Core competencies must be an integrated part of the overall libraries' vision, mission, and strategic planning processes. Core competencies will not succeed if they are considered separate from the overall values of the organization and library.

Conclusions

Core competencies are key elements of the organization's culture and values. These concepts help raise the level of employee knowledge, skill, and abilities by clarifying for the employee and the supervisor the key measures of success. Through core competencies libraries can recruit, hire, train, and retain valuable library staff responsive to the continuously changing library environments. Developing and implementing core competencies touches all parts of the organization. Every staff member and librarian has a stake in the outcomes of discussion about core competencies as these elements become leading factors in how the organization operates. Staff who are not involved in the process are less likely to accept and subsequently practice the concepts.

In today's changing environment, in which libraries are facing multiple competitors for resources and funds and are rapidly incorporating new services and technologies into their organizations, core competencies thoughtfully developed and implemented can provide a solid foundation for organizational change. They provide a road map for staff development programs by identifying key behaviors expected of all employees. The concepts indicate the values the organization rewards and the knowledge and skills needed to be successful. They are an essential part of employee development and pave the way for the library staff to grow and excel in their roles in providing important services to the library clientele.

REFERENCES

ALA's Core Competences of Librarianship. (2008). Approved by ALA's Presidential Task Force on Library Education.

Buttlar, L., & Du Mont, R. (1996). "Library and Information Science Competencies Revisited." Journal of Education for Library and Information Science, 37, 44–62.

Giesecke, J., & McNeil, B. (1999). "Core Competencies and the Learning Organization." Library Administration and Management, 13, 158–166.

Giesecke, J., & McNeil, B. (2004). "Transitioning to the Learning Organization." *Library Trends, 53*, 54–67.

Houghton-Jan, S. (2007). "Technology Competencies and Training for Libraries." *Library Technology Reports, 43*, 29–34.

McNeil, B. (2002). *Core Competencies: A SPEC Kit* (SPEC Kit 270). Washington, DC: Association of Research Libraries.

Ojala, M. (1993). "Core Competencies for Special Library Managers of the Future." *Special Libraries, 84*, 230–234.

Penniman, W. D. (1991, September). "Focusing on Core Competencies." *Journal of Academic Librarianship, 17*, 211–212.

Prahalad, C. K., & Hamel, G. (1990). "The Core Competence of the Corporation." *Harvard Business Review, 68*(3), 79–91.

Robbins, J., & Licona, R. (1994, September–October). "Information Services and Professionals in the Year 2010." *Library Personnel News, 8*, 7–8.

Rockman, I. F., Massey-Burzio, V., & Ritch, A. (1991). "Reference Librarian of the Future." *Reference Services Review, 19*, 71–80.

Shaughnessy, T. W. (1992). "Approaches to Developing Competencies." *Library Trends, 41*, 282–298.

Soutter, J. L. (2007). "Academic Librarian Competency: A Description of Trends in the Peer-Reviewed Journal Literature of 2001–2005." *Partnership: The Canadian Journal of Library and Information Practice and Research, 2*, 1.

Stafford, C. D., & Serban, W. M. (1990). "Core Competencies: Recruiting, Training, and Evaluating in the Automated Reference Environment." *Journal of Library Administration, 13*, 81–97.

Woodsworth, A., & Lester, J. (1991). "Educational Imperatives of the Future Research Library: A Symposium." *Journal of Academic Librarianship, 17*, 204–215.

Woodsworth, A., & Westermann, M. (1995). "Professional Education for Academic Librarians." In G. B. McCabe, & R. J. Person (Eds.), *Academic Libraries: Their Rationale and Role in American Higher Education* (pp. 49–70). Westport, CT: Greenwood Press.

ADDITIONAL RESOURCES

Abels, E., Jones, R., Latham, J., Magnoni, D., & Gard Marshall, J. (2003, June). "Competencies for Information Professionals of the 21st Century" (Rev. ed.). Retrieved from www.sla.org/content/learn/members/competencies/index.cfm

Kochanski, J., & Dillion, B. (1996). "Eight Ways to Create Winning Competencies." *Employment Management Today, 1*(3), 19–23. doi: 10.1002/hrm.3930350102

Mansfield, R. S. (1996). "Building Competency Modes: Approaches for HR Professionals." *Human Resources Management, 35*, 7–18. doi: 10.1002/(SICI)1099-050X(199621)35:1<7::AID-HRM1>3.0.CO;2-2

Reagan, P. M. (1994). "Transform Organizations Using Competency Development." *Journal of Compensation and Benefits, 9*(5), 25–31.

Reference and User Services Association. (2004, June). "Guidelines for Behavioral Performance of Reference and Information Service Providers." Retrieved from www.ala.org/ala/mgrps/divs/rusa/resources/guidelines/guidelines behavioral.cfm

Spencer, L. M., & Spencer, S. M. (1993). *Competence at Work: Models for Superior Performance.* New York, NY: Wiley.

Weech, T. (2007, January). "Competencies Needed for Digital Librarianship." Paper prepared for the Digital Library for the Maghreb Workshop, Rabat, Morocco. Retrieved from www.fulbrightacademy.org/file_depot/0-10000000/20000 -30000/21647/folder/59410/Weech+-+Competencies+needed.pdf

Appendix A

1. List Developed for Initial Twelve Core Competencies

University of Nebraska–Lincoln, University Libraries,
Executive Committee Candidate Interview Questions
Sample interview questions to help determine competency development or the potential for development.

Analytical Skills/Problem Solving/Decision Making

Have you ever had to review proposals submitted by a vendor or by another committee? (Tell me about one of those situations.)

Tell me about a time when you had to analyze or interpret numerical or financial information.

Walk me through a situation in which you had to get information by asking many questions of several people. (How did you know what to ask?)

Give me an example of a time you weren't sure what an internal/external customer wanted. How did you handle the situation?

Think of a good decision you made and a recent decision that wasn't as good. What did you do differently in making those decisions?

Describe a time when you weighed the pros and cons of a situation and decided not to take action, even though you were under pressure to do so.

Your change from _____ to _____ was a major career change. What factors influenced your decision to change jobs?

For New Graduates

What types of information have you used for your career search?

Walk me through a situation in which you had to do research and analyze the results (for school, buying a new car, etc.).

What was the toughest academic decision you had to make? How did you go about making the decision? What alternatives did you consider?

What made you decide to attend _____ (college, library school, training, etc.)?

Communication Skills

How do you keep internal/external customers informed?

Tell me about a recent major directive of management that you had to communicate and implement. How did you go about doing this?

Describe a time you had to ask questions and listen carefully to clarify the exact nature of an internal/external customer's problem.

Creativity/Innovation

In your current position, what have you done differently from your predecessors?

Tell me about a creative idea you had to improve a library service.

Tell me about a unique approach you took to solve a problem.

Give me an example of a new way you were able to apply existing knowledge to solve a problem.

Tell me about the way(s) in which you worked with other staff to develop new and creative ideas to solve problems.

Expertise and Technical Knowledge

What technical training have you received? How did you apply this training?

Describe a project, situation, or assignment that challenged your skills as a _____. What did you do to manage the situation effectively?

Sometimes complex projects require additional expertise. Describe a situation in which you had to request help.

Have you ever had to orient a new employee on a technical task or area? How did you do it?

Describe a time you solved a technical problem.

What equipment have you been trained to operate? How proficient are you?

What word-processing packages can you use? How proficient are you?

Give me an example of a project that demonstrates your technical expertise in _____.

Describe how you've gone about learning a new technical task.

How much experience have you had operating a _____ (mouse, keyboard, typewriter, word processor, etc.)?

Describe the most challenging work you've done.

For New Graduates

Give me an example of an assignment you've worked on that shows your expertise in _____.

Flexibility/Adaptability

Tell me about two of your coworkers who are most different from one another. How have you worked with (or managed to lead) each one? Give me an example.

Working with people from diverse backgrounds or cultures can be a challenge. Can you tell me about a time you faced a challenge adapting to a person from a different background or culture? (What happened? What did you do? What was the result?)

Tell me an important project/task/assignment you were working on in which the specifications changed. (What did you do? How did it affect you?)

Tell me about a time you had to meet a scheduled deadline while your work was being continually interrupted. What caused you to have the most difficulty and why?

Going from _____ (position) to _____ (position) must have been difficult. Tell me about a challenge that occurred when making that transition. (How did you handle it?)

Describe a time you had to significantly modify work procedures to align with new strategic directives.

Tell me about the manager/supervisor who was the most challenging to work for. How did you handle this challenging relationship?

I see that you have moved a number of times. What was the biggest challenge you faced in moving? How did you cope?

Going from (high school to college, college to graduate school, school to your first job) can be a dramatic change. Tell me about a particular challenge you had when you made this transition.

Interpersonal/Group Skills

Tell me about a time you were able to convince someone to cooperate with you on an important project.

Tell me about an experience you've had working with a new employee. Give an example of your dealings what that person.

Sometimes it can be frustrating to try to get information from other people for planning purposes or to solve a problem. Please describe a situation you have had like this.

Our relationships with coworkers are not always perfect. Tell me about the most challenging relationship you had with a coworker. Why was it challenging? What did you do to try to make it work?

Describe a time you worked with a group or team to determine project responsibilities. What was your role?

Can you give an example of a group decision you were involved in recently? What did you do to help the group reach the decision?

Tell me about a situation when a group member disagreed with your ideas or actions.

Tell me about one of the toughest groups you've had to work with. What made it difficult?

Leadership

Sometimes important projects have tight deadlines. Tell me about a time when you had to take action quickly to correct a problem on an important project.

Tell me about a time you inspired someone to work hard to do a good job.

Describe a face-to-face meeting in which you had to lead or influence a very sensitive individual.

Tell me about a time you were able to convince someone from outside (your department, etc.) to cooperate with you on an important project.

What strategies have you used to communicate a major change to employees? Which strategies have worked, and which have not?

Describe a situation in which you had to translate a broad or general plan into specific goals.

For Supervisory Positions

Tell me about a time when you included one of your staff in solving a problem.

Sometimes there's only enough time to tell people what to do and how to do it. Tell me about a time you needed to behave this way with your staff.

Tell me how you established rapport with the newest members of your staff.

Tell me about reward structures or incentives you established to help accomplish a new directive. How did it work?

For New Graduates

Describe a situation in which you had to influence another student or peer to cooperate. What did you say?

Tell me about a leadership role you had in an extracurricular activity. How did you lead?

Organizational Understanding and Global Thinking

Describe a situation in which you chose to involve others to help solve an internal or external customer's problem. (What was the problem? How did involving others help?)

Describe an occasion when you decided to involve others from outside your department in making a decision.

Ownership/Accountability/Dependability

Describe a time when you weighed the pros and cons of a situation and decided not to take action, even though you were under pressure to do so.

We all make decisions that turn out to be mistakes. Describe a work decision you made that you wish you could do over.

Planning and Organizational Skills

Walk me though yesterday (or last week) and tell me how you planned the day's (or week's) activities.

What procedure have you used to keep track of items that need attention? Tell me about a time you used that procedure.

What objectives did you set for this year? (What steps have you taken to make sure that you're making progress on all of them?)

Sometimes deadlines don't allow the luxury of carefully considering all options before making a decision. Please give an example of a time this happened to you. What was the result of your decision?

Tell me about a time you were faced with conflicting priorities. In scheduling your time, how did you determine what was a priority?

For Supervisory Position

Tell me about either a short- or long-term plan you developed for your department.

What strategies have you used to communicate a major new initiative to employees? Which strategies have worked and which have not?

For New Graduates

Tell me about the time your course load was heaviest. How did you complete all your work?

What did you consider when setting up your class schedule?

How were you able to balance your work with extracurricular activities?

Resource Management

Tell me about one of the reward structures or incentives you established to help accomplish a major new directive.

Service Attitude/User Satisfaction

In your current job, how do you know if your internal/external customers are satisfied? (Give a specific example.)

Tell me about a time when you were able to respond to an internal/external customer's request in a shorter period of time than expected. Contrast that situation with a time you failed to meet an internal/external customer's expectations. (What was the difference?)

As a _____, how did you ensure that you were providing good service?

Sometimes it's necessary to work with a customer who has unusual requests. Please describe a time when you had to handle an unusual request that seemed unreasonable. What did you do?

Some days can be very busy with requests from customers and coworkers. Please describe a time recently when you didn't have enough time to completely satisfy a particular customer. How did you handle the situation?

2. Questions Asked during Interview for Candidates for Librarian/Library Faculty Positions

University of Nebraska–Lincoln, University Libraries,
Executive Committee Candidate Interview Questions
Choose one question from each category. Not all the questions in this list are appropriate for every candidate. There may be additional questions you may want to ask in relation to the specific position.

Opening questions:
1. Why are you interested in this position?
2. What strengths would you bring to this position?

Questions specific to the particular position:

Cataloging

MARC format is the classic example of a metadata scheme. Tell us about other metadata schemes with which you are familiar.

Cataloging is a public service. What does this mean to you?

If you were to change the AACR (cataloging code), how would you change it to aid our users?

Liaison Work

As a new liaison librarian, how would you go about making contacts with faculty in your liaison areas?

Describe the impact of new media on collection development or reference activities.

Describe a successful instruction experience you have had as a student or teacher. What about the experience made it successful?

Digital Initiatives

Describe how new media have improved access to historical documents, archives materials, images, audio files, etc.

Describe trends that you see in digitization and how new developments might be effectively applied or utilized in library activities.

Organizational Culture

What elements or characteristics of an organization do you feel are essential?

Describe a working environment in which you would thrive.

Please give us an idea of your ideal working environment.

What would you say is the most important thing you are looking for in a job?

Creativity/Innovation

Describe a project, situation, or assignment where you were creative or innovative.

What role do you feel creativity or innovation plays in today's library?

What would you consider to be your most creative or innovative achievement? Why?

Time Management: Establishing Priorities

What do you do when work priorities change quickly? Give us an example of when this happened.

How do you manage multiple priorities and conflicting deadlines?

How do you ensure that projects get completed on deadline, particularly if priorities change or new information comes to light that complicates the project?

Management Style

Describe the amount of structure, direction, and feedback that you prefer? What motivates you to put forth your best effort?

SUPERVISORY POSITION: How would you describe your management style?

SUPERVISORY POSITION: As a manager, how do you solicit input?

SUPERVISORY POSITION: As a supervisor, how do you prefer to communicate with your unit or department?

How would you gather input in a situation where a decision had to be made, yet procedures or policies were not in place to govern the situation?

Learning Organization

How would you go about learning your new position at the UNL Libraries?

What do you think would be the most challenging aspect of this position for you?

Please give me an example of how you adapt to change.

Diversity/Generational

Tell us about a time that you adapted your approach in order to work effectively with someone from a different culture or generation.

How do you ensure that diverse viewpoints are voiced, considered, and represented when gathering input and making decisions?

When conversing with someone from a different culture or generation, how do you ensure that you clearly understand his or her viewpoint?

If you were in a work situation where it was important for you to share a viewpoint different from the majority, how would you go about sharing that viewpoint?

"The University of Nebraska–Lincoln (UNL) seeks to achieve a working and learning environment that is open to all people. Diversity is one hallmark of great institutions of learning and has long been one of the strengths of our society." What is your responsibility in making this happen? What is the library's responsibility? (Source: UNL EEO statement, April 2005; http://hr.unl.edu/employment/employment01 .shtml#eeo.)

"Dignity and respect for all in the UNL community is the responsibility of each individual member of the community. The realization of that responsibility across the campus is critical to UNL's success." What is your role in making this happen? What is the library's role? (Source: UNL EEO statement, April 2005; http://hr.unl.edu/employment/ employment01.shtml#eeo.)

Please describe how diversity or inclusive initiatives make a difference in a work environment.

Project Management/Resource Management

Describe a recent instance where the resources were not adequate to fully fund a project or activity. What changes did you make to the project to work within the budget or to seek alternative funding?

SUPERVISORY POSITION: Tell us about a project or workflow that spanned more than one unit or department. How did you contribute to developing and maintaining an effective working relationship with the other unit?

If you were given leadership of a complex librarywide project and told to investigate, develop policies and procedures, then implement it how would you go about carrying out this mandate?

Teamwork

How do you get people with different viewpoints to establish a common or collaborative approach to a problem? Give us a recent example.

Describe an instance where you had to enlist support/participation of staff from another department for your work.

Supervision

As a supervisor, how do you get staff motivated to work on a project?

Describe a successful working relationship between a supervisor and an employee.

TENURE TRACK POSITION: Give us your view of the importance of tenure.

This position would require that you are active in scholarly and creative activities such as research, publication, presentations, and grant writing. What areas of research interest you?

Please describe your experience with scholarly activities such as research, publication, presentations, and grant writing.

Closing Questions:

Is there any other information you think is helpful and that you would like us to consider?

Are there any questions you would like to ask us?

3. Early Handout Developed for Human Resources to Explain Core Competencies to Applicants for Staff Positions in the Library

University of Nebraska–Lincoln, University Libraries

The University Libraries strives to be a learning organization, where we create, acquire, and transfer knowledge and ideas, and modify behaviors to reflect new knowledge and insights. As part of this effort, the Libraries have developed a list of twelve core competencies that contribute to an individual's success as a staff member of the University Libraries.

Core Competencies

- Analytical skills/problem solving/decision making
- Communication skills
- Creativity/innovation
- Expertise and technical knowledge
- Flexibility/adaptability
- Interpersonal/group skills
- Leadership
- Organizational understanding and group thinking
- Ownership/accountability/dependability
- Planning and organizational skills

- Resource management
- Service attitude/user satisfaction

Here are some examples of the types of questions relating to the Libraries' core competencies that you might be asked during your upcoming interview:

> Walk me through a situation in which you had to get information by asking many questions of several people. How did you know what to ask?
>
> Describe a time you had to ask questions and listen carefully to clarify the exact nature of an internal/external customer's problem.
>
> Tell me about a way in which you worked with other staff to develop creative ideas to solve problems.
>
> Describe how you've gone about learning a new technical task.
>
> Describe the most challenging work you've done.
>
> Tell me about a time you had to meet a scheduled deadline while your work was being continually interrupted. What caused you to have the most difficulty?
>
> Can you give me an example of a group decision you were involved in recently? What did you do to help the group reach the decision?
>
> What procedure have you used to keep track of items that need attention? Tell me about a time you used that procedure.
>
> Walk me through yesterday and tell me how you planned the day's activities.
>
> In your current position, how do you ensure that you are providing good service?
>
> Sometimes it is necessary to work with a customer who has unusual requests. Please describe a time when you had to handle an unusual request that seemed unreasonable. What did you do?

Jeanne F. Voyles and Robyn Huff-Eibl

chapter 8

How Understanding the Organization, Clear Expectations, and Competencies Lead to Successful Coaching and Performance

THIS CHAPTER PRESENTS A DIFFERENT APPROACH TO COACHING. The focus is on how understanding the organization, hiring for specific competencies, written performance expectations, and coaching, combined with an effective performance system, can create satisfying and effective job performance for both the employee and the organization. Although coaching has traditionally been used to improve job performance, the identification of competencies and performance expectations provide a more transparent environment for the employee. There are a variety of approaches that supervisors, managers, and coworkers can follow when coaching library staff, which includes both classified staff and librarians, to be successful in their positions. Here is our definition of coaching from the University of Arizona Library (UAL): coaching involves you or a subject expert in informal one-on-one or small group instruction at the point when a performance (new ability, improvement, or behavior) is desired or necessary.

Dennis C. Kinlaw (1999) defines successful coaching as a mutual conversation that follows a predictable process and leads to superior performance, commitment to sustained improvement, and positive relations. Kinlaw believes that coaching is an alternative to managing performance by trying to control people. He states that people achieve and sustain superior performance when "(1) they have greater clarity about their goals and their importance, (2) they can exert influence over their goals, (3) they are more competent to achieve their goals, and (4) they receive more appreciation for working tirelessly to achieve these goals" (Kinlaw, 1999, p. 5). The coaching process that Kinlaw (1999) describes encompasses four stages: involving (clear expectations, comfort, and trust), developing (information, insight, and learning), resolving (closure, next steps, positive relationships, and commitment), and initiating alternatives.

UAL has adopted much of Kinlaw's philosophy regarding coaching. At the University of Arizona many factors are in place to ensure that all library staff receive the support needed to meet the expectations and competencies defined for their position. The use of competencies is an opportunity to realize greater efficiency and effectiveness by implementing competency requirements. Hiring for specific competency-based job descriptions, which reflect current and future competencies, and presenting well-defined performance expectations, along with successful coaching, creates a combination that leads to a win-win situation for the individual and the organization, and especially the customer.

Understanding the Organization

At the University of Arizona we orient new employees to librarywide philosophy and values in addition to work expectations. The basic understanding of what we define as an effective team member occurs early on at the functional team or home team where the staff person was hired or assigned. The team leader coaches to the expectations and competencies defined for the library staff position.

LIBRARY STAFF EXPECTATIONS

The library is an agile and innovative, team-based organization committed to continuous learning, increasing customer self-sufficiency, and fostering a diverse environment. Our mission includes furthering cultural transmission by using cost-effective methods for acquiring, curating, managing, and connecting customers to information services and resources and providing education in their use.

Individuals can expect that their work will include team and librarywide work (e.g., process improvement teams, meetings, planning and implementation projects, strategic long-range planning). As customers' needs change, our work requirements or patterns change. As a result, team and library work is negotiated in the team, the end product being an agreement in writing represented by each staff's performance and learning goals, as evaluated by a regular performance appraisal.

Each team member is responsible for the following (an asterisk indicates concepts taken from Goleman, 1998):

- Understanding and communicating the vision, mission, and priorities of the library and the team(s) to move the library and team(s) to their goals
- Understanding and demonstrating commitment toward the "Library Values":
    Customer focus
    Continuous improvement and learning
    Diversity
    Integrity
    Flexibility
- Participating in the planning and decision-making processes for customer service, which includes making customers and their needs a primary focus and readjusting priorities to respond to pressing and changing customer demands
- Accepting change and exhibiting flexibility and adaptability in working in teams and dealing with team and librarywide issues and concerns
- Ability to work effectively with and support others in a diverse team-based environment
- Exhibiting emotional intelligence skills in interpersonal relations, such as courtesy, self-control, active listening, empathy, optimism, and conflict management*
- Attending and participating in team meetings and projects as assigned and facilitating and leading meetings as needed
- Ability to seek information and constructively respond to feedback related to learning or performing your work and the work of the team
- Demonstrating respect for all colleagues regardless of race, gender, disability, lifestyle, or viewpoint

- Solving as many of their own problems as possible; resolving issues close to the action rather than passing responsibility for solutions to others and being empowered to do so
- Making decisions at the appropriate level and, when working with others, utilizing appropriate decision-making processes
- Exhibiting truthfulness, conscientiousness, and initiative*
- Self-awareness, including fair evaluation of one's performance, career path, and opportunities*
- Reflecting on one's performance and actively striving to improve*
- Prioritizing work, and self-monitoring and correcting as necessary*
- Maintaining a customer service orientation and service orientation to the library, which includes presenting a professional, cheerful, and positive manner and quickly and effectively solving customer problems
- Effective communication at all levels, which involves the ability to put aside one's own views, beliefs, and judgments to listen and understand what others say and mean (suspending judgment and active listening); the ability to express your point of view, beliefs, assumptions, feelings, wants, and needs without discounting the beliefs, and so on, of others (advocacy and assertiveness); and stating what leads you to think, believe, or feel the way you do by using concrete data that is the basis for the conclusions you have reached
- Ability to give and accept constructive criticism using the Constructive Dialogue process
- Challenging self and colleagues to think creatively and broadly
- Willingness and ability to develop others in your area of expertise*
- Willingness to accept assignments outside of your primary work responsibilities that are appropriate to your skills or important to your learning
- Serving as change catalyst when appropriate*

New Employee Orientation

As our organization has evolved so has our New Employee Orientation (NEO) program. Since 2007, attendance of this program is required for all new library staff and is included in all hiring contracts. This program presents to staff an orientation to our library values, principles of the organization, the concept of systems thinking, and a closer look at what it means to work in a team-based organization. All new library staff receive the *New Employee Orientation Notebook*. There are five NEO foundation sessions. Presenting this foundation for new staff begins the journey of building commitment to the values of the organization and emphasizes accountability. Employees can then practice what they learn and apply it in a variety of team experiences throughout the team and organization, from functional team projects to cross-functional library-wide team projects on an individual basis.

The six foundational components of the NEO program include the following:

1. "The Big Picture" (introduction and History of UAL team-based organization)
2. "The U of A Library Structure, Processes, and Systems"
3. "Working in Teams"
4. "Team-Based Foundations" and the Myers-Briggs Type Inventory
5. "Facilitation of Effective Meetings and Decision Making"
6. "Creating Respectful Workplaces"

For new employees there is a relationship with what they learn during the NEO sessions and our performance effectiveness management system (PEMS). This further connects the concept of systems thinking as one objective for new employees to be able to view the organization as a whole system rather than as separate independent units or individuals. It is important for new employees to understand how staff and units interact and are interrelated and interdependent. For new employees, the team leader, supervisor, colleague, or individual can develop goals, expectations, and competencies. We believe that creating a clear performance appraisal document leads to strong performance and supports an effective coaching process. The individual learns about PEMS through the NEO sessions, coaching sessions, and through observation of staff practicing what it is to work in a team.

EXPECTATIONS AND COMPETENCIES

When creating a performance appraisal document, one approach is to define the goal and define success (figure 8.1). Although providing feedback on individual performance evaluations is important, it is far more critical to define up front the competencies and goals required of an employee. Success can be related to specific defined outcomes and corroborated through behaviors that others will observe and that the individual will demonstrate. This allows the employee to focus on overall outcomes rather than outputs. It also provides context for the behaviors and competencies an organization can expect of each employee. As new employees are hired, supervisors review competencies identified during the hiring process and competencies that were not identified. This allows the supervisor to assess overall competencies of an individual and to develop appropriate performance goals as necessary. All goals that include performance toward team and library strategic planning processes require individual quality standards to be embedded in the goal and work expectations. Each team member documents his or her progress during the designated time period for a review.

Figure 8.1: Performance Review: Example Goal, Library Operations Supervisor

Performance Review: Example Goal, Library Operations Supervisor

**PERFORMANCE GOAL NO. 3
(COACHING AND MENTORING SERVICE SITE STAFF):**

Coach and mentor, using the "Competencies and Work Team Leader Expectations" document, six Access and Information Services team members in the Service Sites work team to ensure that work is accomplished in an appropriate and timely manner and that staff has the competencies they need to complete their functional assignments.

If I am successful in accomplishing this goal, the outcome will be:

☐ Making progress on staff goals, including providing assistance in developing staff learning and performance goals, setting performance measures, setting quality and quantity standards, and removing barriers to accomplish goals

☐ Initiating and documenting communication with library staff regarding patterns of errors, behavior, and/or strong and consistent performance

☐ Staff providing a higher level of performance review feedback to their peers, specifically asking probing questions and providing constructive feedback

☐ Scheduling and completing performance reviews on time

☐ Coaching staff on application for career progression and/or merit

☐ Mentoring and advising on opportunities for career development, involvement in programs or associations (e.g., ALA, Arizona Library Association, Tri-University Meetings, Innovative Interfaces User Group Meeting)

☐ Building positive working relationships among Service Site staff, across the entire team and librarywide

☐ Leading dialogues and initiating meetings with library staff on policy changes, process changes, and new services using effective meetings, problem solving, and decision making and facilitation

☐ Providing timely feedback (e.g., performance issues, accomplishments, kudos)

☐ Facilitating weekly meetings with staff (including preparing an agenda ahead of time; leading the meeting; and making sure minutes, decisions, and assigned responsibilities are tracked and communicated with all)

☐ Planning in advance for peak workloads and vacations

☐ Communicating in a timely manner with Service Site staff on any changes in work processes or any other relevant information (e.g., updates from Access and Information Services Leadership Team, library administration, or librarywide project teams)

☐ Ensuring communication between team members and the entire team (and librarywide if appropriate) when there are limited resources to meet quality standards

☐ Staff understanding library competencies and how they apply to them and their colleagues, and staff exhibiting library- and job-specific competencies when performing their work

☐ Staff understanding how to plan and expend budgets in desired spending patterns

☐ Ensuring adherence to Access and Information Services Team and librarywide work expectations

☐ Demonstrating knowledge of university's and library's human resources policies and procedures

Evidence that will corroborate my performance and behaviors and/or demonstrations that others will observe include the following:

☐ I will provide challenging, corrective, supportive, and encouraging feedback on goals and progress toward those goals for each staff member whom I supervise during each review period and in between as needed.

☐ As opportunities for career development arise, I will share this information with any person who will benefit from the opportunity.

☐ I will always make myself available in a timely manner to help with the removal of barriers and with problem solving.

☐ I have the skills necessary to aid in the development of my colleagues and to engage as a mentor and demonstrate ability to identify contacts and/or groups that will inform or develop my mentee.

☐ I will assist an individual link his or her longer-term goals with current assignments.

☐ I will develop a deeper understanding of coaching and mentoring competencies and skills.

☐ I will demonstrate ability to hire, train, and supervise staff on the basis of library-established competencies.

☐ I will provide opportunities to practice and gain experience and competencies.

Milestone 1: Coach, mentor and supervise six staff through weekly meetings as well as providing feedback on performance reviews. Create mentoring plans toward meeting future goals and/or coaching plans for staff regarding inconsistencies in their performance.

Milestone 2: Provide performance review feedback to Service Site staff (and other librarywide staff as required) and ensure that reviews are completed within established deadlines. Conduct year-end performance evaluations (due May 2009) for each staff member who I supervise (including documenting accomplishments and areas in which improvements are needed and/or focus for upcoming year).

Milestone 3: Review budget on a monthly basis with individuals whom I supervise and any onetime project money. Analysis of spending patterns will lead us to develop a plan of action to be taken to get back on track if the budget is more than 1 percent under- or overspent; this could include reallocation of the budget. It is also expected that the supervisor will work with staff members on development of upcoming fiscal year budget requests, which are due to the team leader on April 1.

Milestone 4:	Ensure that I am aware of and conversant in Access and Information Service teamwork expectations and library and university human resources policies.
Milestone 5:	Attend and complete University Leadership Institute courses and Capstone Experience to further develop my leadership skills (www .hr.arizona.edu/08_o/development3/programInfo/index.php?prog =uli&sel=summa). This institute is designed to strengthen competencies identified by the hiring authorities at the University of Arizona as essential for peak performance and builds community and supports the creation of informal professional support networks. Not only does the program provide leadership practice, it gives me an opportunity to network with others on campus and learn more in-depth about the various areas of campus and university acumen.

Successful Coaching Leads to High Levels of Performance

STRATEGIES FOR SUCCESSFUL COACHING

- Create an environment of learning, not fear.
- Assess the area that needs coaching, and engage in a conversation with staff.
- Identify clearly and be specific about the competency or performance area to improve or achieve.
- Identify the capability of staff to achieve the competency. What knowledge, skills, and abilities are already present that indicate that employees can learn and achieve the desired outcome?
- Engage staff in creating the plan to achieve the competency. Ask questions like, "What would help you become more proficient?" and "What thoughts or ideas do you have to achieve the goal?"
- Identify strategies that support staff to achieve the outcome. Write milestones to be included in the performance appraisal document that are indicators that staff is making progress.
- Identify key staff who can provide training and specific feedback, and are knowledgeable in the competency to be accomplished. Ask the person being coached, "Which colleague(s) would you identify to help you achieve the goal?"

- Encourage staff to invite constructive feedback from members of the team on specific outcomes or behaviors that demonstrate the desired outcome. Coaching can come from many different directions, from the team leader and project team leader to individuals on the team.
- Give the library staff an opportunity to practice and gain experience.
- Check in consistently that the individual is making progress toward the goal. Ask staff what is working, what isn't working, and whether there are other strategies to employ to help the employee achieve success.
- Document behaviors and outcomes that demonstrate that staff have made progress or demonstrated competency.
- Identify barriers that may keep staff from fully achieving the goals. Ask staff to identify these barriers, then problem solve together on removing any barriers.
- Highlight their success, small or large. Reassure staff that they can achieve success. Appreciate their commitment to achieve the competency.

ASSESSING COACHING SKILLS OF EMPLOYEES

Learning to give constructive feedback takes practice and time. After attending Constructive Dialogue training developed by Dances with Opportunity (2002), one of the mechanisms that the University of Arizona uses to help staff learn to perform this task is to participate on a performance appraisal review in which someone new gives feedback. The team leader or supervisor listens to the feedback given by the new employee. After the performance review is over, the team leader or supervisor schedules a meeting with the reviewer to provide feedback on the employee's coaching performance. The employee providing feedback documents what he or she has learned in a goal with expectations clearly defined (figure 8.2).

Effective coaching builds commitment to the organization. Coaching is a two-way relationship. The more the employee is engaged in the process, the more successful the employee is in achieving high performance.

Learning and Performance Goal: Providing coaching and constructive feedback during the Developmental Review Process

This goal will assist in my ability to be an effective peer reviewer during the developmental review process by giving positive and constructive feedback particularly in the areas for which I was selected to be a review member. I will also meet with my supervisor to review my feedback after each review period.

If the supervisor is successful in accomplishing this goal, the outcomes will be the following:

☐ Staff will receive feedback that will aid in their development, learning, and performance.

☐ Staff will value my participation as a review member.

☐ I will learn and demonstrate techniques involved in asking probing questions and providing both positive and constructive feedback.

Behaviors and/or demonstrations that others will observe include the following:

☐ I will document the feedback that I have given during each review on which I serve so that my supervisor can provide me input on my feedback.

☐ Staff will observe me asking probing questions and providing supportive and constructive feedback.

Milestone 1: Complete Constructive Dialogue training.

Milestone 2: Identify the specific areas for which I was selected to provide feedback as a peer reviewer.

Milestone 3: Review with supervisor or team leader key concepts for providing effective performance review feedback (see figure 8.3).

Milestone 4: Read performance appraisal document before meeting with individual being reviewed. Schedule meeting with supervisor or team leader to discuss areas in which I will provide feedback.

Milestone 5: During each performance review, provide feedback to colleague. After each performance review, schedule meeting with supervisor or team leader to discuss feedback. Document what has been learned from session and incorporate changes into upcoming performance review meetings.

Milestone 6: Capture feedback on my performance from other members of the performance appraisal team.

Key Concepts for Providing Effective Performance Review Feedback

GENERAL TIPS

☐ Do not focus on spelling or grammar issues, unless the information is not understandable.

☐ Positive feedback involves telling someone about good performance. Make this feedback timely, specific, and frequent.

☐ Clearly define and articulate feedback by using specific examples, data, or facts.

☐ Ask probing or clarifying questions if information is not understood.

☐ If no barriers or problems are presented, ask thought-provoking questions to encourage reflection that leads to growth and continual improvement. Individuals should be demonstrating professional growth and development achieved through relevant continuing education and learning activities.

☐ Check to make sure that the other person understood what you communicated by using a feedback loop, such as asking a question or observing changed behavior.

☐ Allow for discussion on topics as needed.

☐ Center support and encouragement on what works well using the appreciative inquiry approach, which analyzes problems occurring and what is working (Hammond, 1998).

☐ The main purpose of constructive feedback is to help people understand where they stand in relation to expected and/or productive job behavior.

☐ The best feedback is sincerely and honestly provided to help.

☐ Recognition for effective performance is a powerful motivator. Most people want to obtain more recognition, so recognition fosters more of the appreciated actions.

☐ Look to see how an individual is demonstrating librarywide competencies that we look for in all staff:

- ability to work effectively with others in a diverse team-based environment
- flexibility and ability to grow and contribute in a changing environment
- effective communication at all levels
- analytical skills and ability to contribute new thoughts and participate in collaborative problem solving and decision making
- creativity, originality, and ingenuity in the many technical and human situations encountered in library work

- ability to accept and delegate authority and responsibility, including taking leadership roles in library work
- ability to give and accept constructive criticism
- independence of judgment and initiative
- willingness to contribute to the planning and decision-making processes where appropriate

DISCUSSING OUTPUTS AND OUTCOMES

☐ Feedback is focused on modifiable behavior and meaningful outcomes, not on assigning blame.

☐ Constructive feedback alerts an individual to an area in which his or her performance could improve. Constructive feedback is not criticism; it is descriptive and should always focus on specific behavior, not on a person or his or her intentions.

☐ Did the individual describe their consistency as work performance?

☐ What is the service or product the individual is providing that is new or that he or she has never done before?

☐ What activities did the applicant initiate, influence, or implement?

☐ Did the individual talk about the impact those activities had on the team or the customers? Did the individual describe the impact in terms of what has changed for the better, and for whom?

☐ Did the individual describe how the impact was created and the individual's contribution to making it happen—did he or she distinguish between what the team accomplished and what he or she did specifically to help the team with its accomplishments?

☐ Was the individual specific in describing the following?
- What they accomplished
- New work, assignments, responsibilities
- Accomplishments that clearly illustrate new levels of ability and/or commitment
- Accomplishments in which the applicant's contribution amid a larger group effort is clear
- How they accomplished it
- Why the accomplishment was needed
- What the applicant contributed, such as actions that illustrate achievement to any or all of the criteria of career progression
- Specifically how the accomplishment was achieved (e.g., "I promoted diversity" is more specific than "I created a project to hire minority

student employees for the desk"), which can be further specified in terms of how the project was created

- Who was involved
- When it occurred
- Where it fit into the larger scheme of things
- What the (before and after) result was
- Specific qualities or quantities of change in capability, practice, or production
- Customer responses to the change
- Changes in number, percentage, frequency, volume, or measures of time
- Indications of the importance or consequence of the achievement
- Outcomes for customers or the team that are linked to team goals or standards
- Evidence of a causal relationship between the achievement and actions or events downstream (e.g., providing training to colleagues (causes) that increased confidence and use of new software (causes) and new approaches to service delivery (resulting in) increased customer satisfaction)—rather than trying to prove that the training caused an increase in customer satisfaction, try to show how the training is related as one of many causes

DISCUSSING HOW TO GIVE DIFFICULT FEEDBACK

☐ Do not avoid tough issues; timely feedback is best.

☐ Whenever possible, feedback that is requested is more powerful. Ask permission to provide feedback. Say, "I'd like to give you some feedback about the presentation, is that OK with you?"

☐ Effective feedback involves what or how something was done, not why. Asking why is asking people about their motivation, which provokes defensiveness.

☐ Use problem-solving processes that lead to sustainable results.

☐ Develop action plans or next steps that have obtainable and measurable outcomes.

☐ Use strategies for responding to strong emotions and reactions.

- If you are concerned about the impact of your feedback, consider asking a trusted colleague to read the feedback before you send it as a test of whether the tone you intend to send is what is in fact communicated.
- Example: "It would be helpful if this person could be better supported by her team." The tone is gentle but doesn't communicate with any

strength the underlying concern. Is lack of support a problem caused by the person or the team?

- Example: "This person will never get what she wants from the team." The tone is harsh. Words like *never* are loaded with cynicism.

☐ Confront and resolve challenging issues while maintaining mutual respect; be specific about what you saw, felt, or experienced and what you want more of.

- Example: "This person isn't very accountable" (fuzzy).

- Example: "This person on two occasions decided to change procedures without consulting with the team" (specific).

- Example: "I would suggest in the future that this person bring changes he or she is considering to the attention of the team leader for possible placement on the team agenda."

- Supplement belief statements, conclusions, assumptions, and meanings you associate with observable facts.

- Example: "I believe he or she is not serious about improving work processes" (belief).

- Example: "I believe he or she is not serious about improving work processes, because I have twice made suggestions for improvements without any positive response" (belief plus observation).

REFERENCES

Kinlaw, D. C. (1999). *Coaching for Commitment: Interpersonal Strategies for Obtaining Superior Performance from Individuals and Teams.* San Francisco: Jossey-Bass/Pfeiffer.

Goleman, D. (1998). *Working with Emotional Intelligence.* New York, NY: Bantam Books.

Hammond, S. A. (1998). *The Thin Book of Appreciative Inquiry* (2nd ed.). Plano, TX: Thin Book Publishing Company.

ADDITIONAL RESOURCES

Balestracci, D. (2003). "Handling the Human Side of Change." *Change Management, 36*(11), 38–46.

Berens, L. V., Ernst, L. K., & Smith, M. A. (2004). *Quick Guide to the 16 Personality Types and Teams: Applying Team Essentials to Create Effective Teams.* Huntington Beach, CA: Telos.

Dances with Opportunity. (2002). "Facilitating Constructive Dialogue Workbook." Tucson, AZ: Author. Retrieved from www.danceswithopportunity.com

Markle, G. L. (2000). *Catalytic Coaching: The End of the Performance Review.* Westport, CT: Quorum Books.

Metz, R. F. (2002). *Coaching in the Library: A Management Strategy for Achieving Excellence.* Chicago, IL: American Library Association.

Myers, I. B. (1998). *Introduction to Type: A Guide to Understanding Your Results on the Myers-Briggs Type Indicator.* Mountain View, CA: Consulting Psychologist Press.

Pegasus Communications. "What is Systems Thinking?" Retrieved from http://thesystems thinker.com/systemsthinkinglearn.html

Senge, P. M., Kleiner, A., Roberts, C., Ross, R. B., & Smith, B. J. (1994). *The Fifth Discipline Fieldbook: Strategies and Tools for Building a Learning Organization.* New York, NY: Doubleday Dell.

Stone, D., Patton, B., & Heen, S. (1999). *Difficult Conversations: How to Discuss What Matters Most.* New York, NY: Penguin Group.

University of Arizona, University Leadership Institute. (N.d.). "ULI Program Summary." Retrieved from www.hr.arizona.edu/08_0/development3/programInfo/index.php?prog=uli&sel=summa

University of Arizona Library. (N.d.). "New Employee Orientation (NEO) Foundation Sessions." Retrieved from http://intranet.library.arizona.edu/teams/hroe/neo/NEOFoundations.html

Jeanne F. Voyles and Robyn Huff-Eibl

chapter 9

Cross-Functional Training and Collaboration within the Organization

THIS CHAPTER FOCUSES ON THE STRATEGIES TO APPLY WHEN training staff to work on cross-functional project teams, which will lead to successful collaboration and the organization achieving its mission and vision.

At the University of Arizona cross-functional teams are used to achieve performance that a single individual could not otherwise achieve. The cross-functional teams represent a cross-section of library staff (both librarians and classified staff) in the organization. There are two types of cross-functional teams: standing (ongoing teams that are continuously staffed, with rotating members focused on making recommendations and managing process) and project (members across the library form a team to solve a problem or initiate a new service, and then hand off any ongoing work to permanent teams and dissolve). A project team's work has a beginning and an end. At least one member of the team has completed project management training and applies that methodology when leading or working as a member of the team. Learning and applying effective project management gives the team and its members a foundation that will guide them through the life of the project.

Components of Project Planning and Management Training

As resource constraints are becoming tighter and we face both financial and workload barriers, it is essential that we effectively understand and manage projects with clear resource implications, deadlines, and outcomes. It is critical that organizations fully comprehend the purpose, constraints, risks, and support implementation of complex initiatives and projects without overburdening the human and financial resources of the library. At the University of Arizona we have adopted the Brigham Young University (BYU) model of project planning and management, with some local modifications (Brigham Young University Enterprise Project Management Office, 2005; University of Arizona Library, 2008). Ernie Nielsen, assistant vice president for information technology and managing director of enterprise services portfolio management at BYU, was selected as a training consultant. The BYU model includes three phases:

1. Preplanning—Establish the project context, review project information, and establish the planning structure.
2. Planning—Plan the project by defining and validating the project scope, and by creating a preliminary resource and project schedule; create a work breakdown structure; reconcile the existing plan against project objectives; create a risk management plan; and obtain confirmation and support to proceed.
3. Implementation—Execute the plan, manage the project by documenting and reporting on project performance using meaningful timelines that are legitimate accountability tools, and transfer stewardship to the appropriate unit for integration into ongoing work processes.

The BYU model defines a project as "a single bounded effort with a defined beginning, a defined end, a specific deliverable and a budget" (Brigham Young University Enterprise Project Management Office, 2005, p. G15).

For project management to be effective, it is important for employees to understand the various project management roles. An administrative group reviews project proposals for approval. Once approved, a project sponsor is appointed. The project sponsor is a ranking member of the organization's executive group who will assign and work with a project manager to further define the scope of the project. Responsibilities of a project sponsor include the following:

- Compiling and providing context and background information to project manager and planning team, including a project objective statement of twenty-five or fewer words (e.g., create a prototype for an online one-unit credit course for information literacy in biology [scope], and test by June 17, 2009 [schedule], using 1.5 FTE librarian time [resources])
- Providing constraint matrix and timelines (if timelines are non-negotiable; otherwise the work breakdown structure should produce the timeline); for example:

	Scope	Resources	Timeline
Least		X	
Moderate	X		
Most			X

- Validating scope and providing success criteria to the project manager and planning team (figure 9.1)
- Assisting the project manager in identifying and appointing project team members who have a complementary mix of skills (technical or functional experts, problem-solving and decision-making skills, and interpersonal or team management skills)
- Monitoring progress of the project and reviewing and signing off at designated points in project process, including giving or denying permission to continue the project, providing final approval to finalize a project plan before transitioning into project implementation, and making final decisions regarding unresolved conflicts

The project manager monitors, investigates, takes action, and reports on performance (MITAR). The project manager focuses on providing facilitative leadership and has the ability to lead and manage group and interpersonal dynamics to accomplish work in a timely manner. It is recommended that this person is not the technical expert. Responsibilities of a project manager include the following:

- Gathering and reviewing project information to identify missing or unclear information

- Planning and holding Stargate meetings, during which the project sponsor validates approach, progress, and changes at each identified stage of the process
- Working with the planning team to create the "Definition Document" (see figure 9.1) and governance framework, which is the agreement on policies and procedures that guide the project
- Training the planning team on appropriate processes and tools as needed, including the work breakdown structure and risk management plan for contingencies if needed
- Creating the preliminary project schedule, including assigning task owners and developing estimates of time required for work
- Reconciling existing plan and project objectives, and ultimately seeking confirmation and support of the plan
- Identifying and managing issues, risks, and changes by monitoring project documentation and the environment and contrasting planned activities with actual performance and outcome
- Reporting weekly progress, including problems or delays, to the project sponsor
- Overseeing that all stewardships and responsibilities pass from the project team to the organization (shared responsibility with project sponsor)

The project-planning team and subsequent implementation team complete steps outlined in the planning and implementation stages. Members will be appointed on the basis of criteria specific to the project. Responsibilities of project members include the following:

- Being available for project meetings and participating fully in the work of the project team
- Assisting in developing estimates of time required to accomplish tasks one is assigned
- Accepting roles on the project and report progress on assigned tasks on agreed-on schedule
- Notifying project manager whenever problems arise affecting one's work that may delay the completion of a task or delay the project

Definition Document

OBJECTIVE STATEMENT

Develop an implementation plan by April 30, 2009, that will result in the de-selection and movement of Fine Arts, Center for Creative Photography, Science-Engineering, and possibly Main Library collections, furniture, and equipment to or within Science-Engineering Library by July 31, 2009. (University of Arizona Library, 2009.)

ORGANIZATIONAL SUCCESS CRITERIA

Develop an implementation plan by April 30, 2009, that meets all major deadlines, addresses all of the scope parameters, and is approved by cabinet.

PROJECT INTERDEPENDENCIES

☐ Actually moving materials may be dependent on Arizona Board of Regents' (ABOR) decision regarding student fee increase.

☐ Decision about what to do with compact shelving from Fine Arts will need to be made before any other decisions (how much to deselect and where materials move to in Science-Engineering Library).

☐ University Information Technology Services (UITS) will need to complete any work on wiring and ports before the move.

☐ If Center for Creative Photography (CCP) material is paged rather than moved, we will need to have process for paging materials from Media Arts worked so the two paging schedules can mesh.

☐ Decision about where all Fine Arts and CCP materials needs to be made before we move any materials.

PROJECT DELIVERABLES AND COMPLETION CRITERIA

D1: Develop two facilities plans (all noncomputer equipment, furniture, utilities infrastructure, storage), including identifying onetime request for funds and not including a onetime request for funds.

D2: Develop a deselection plan (collections materials).

D3: Develop a space plan (linear footage for shelving, office, student use, fire and Americans with Disabilities Act codes).

D4: Develop two information technology plans (computers and equipment), including identifying onetime request for funds and not including a onetime request for funds.

D5: Develop two physical-move-of-materials plans (collections from Fine Arts, CCP, and possibly Main to new location), including identifying onetime request for funds and not including a onetime request for funds.

D6: Develop a list of possible digitization opportunities.

D7: Develop a recommendation about access to materials during the implementation phase.

EXAMPLE COMPLETION CRITERIA FOR DELIVERABLE 1

D1: Develop two facilities plans (all noncomputer equipment, furniture, utilities infrastructure, storage), including identifying onetime request for funds and not including a onetime request for funds.

REQUIREMENTS

Is About	Is Not About
Planning safety and security, fire, and Americans with Disabilities Act compliance	New furniture
Planning the how and when and where furniture will be disassembled and reassembled	This team doing any of the physical work
Planning the coordination of Xerox photocopier moves	Doing the physical installation of electrical outlets
Planning the proper amount of electricity and outlets are available	This team physically moving the photocopiers
Planning the dismantling of compact shelving and related costs	This team doing the actual physical move
Planning the moving of Fine Arts Library listening stations and Fine Arts Library audiovisual equipment	Moving CCP furniture or Rare Book Room or CCP audiovisual equipment (all stays at CCP)
Planning Research Support Services, other staff, and National Flute Association student office equipment locations	Cleaning or repairing the space after we have left the Fine Arts Library
Planning for the storage of extra equipment	

- Two plan documents are created: one that includes onetime costs and one that has no costs.
- Facilities director has a written list of standards for legal compliance that will be shared with the implementation team and that the team must follow.
- Any items to be moved that are under warranty or under maintenance agreements will be identified as needing onetime funds and identified as loss if warranty is broken.
- Any equipment and furniture not under warranty will be identified for moving by library facilities team.
- Storage space will be identified.
- A cost estimate for facilities infrastructure will be obtained from university facilities.
- Sponsors and cabinet will approve one of the plans.

For a staff member to be successful on a project team or collaborating in the organization, expectations needs to be clear to the individual. What is expected of members of a project team? What is expected of the project manager of a team or library project? At the University of Arizona Library (UAL), members of project teams have specific goals written as part of our Performance Effective Management System (PEMS). (University of Arizona Library, 2009.)

Elements to consider when writing goals for the project manager include the following:

☐ Successfully leading the project team to achieve the team charge

☐ Following project management principles and process throughout the project

☐ Applying effective meeting practices and facilitation

☐ Using constructive dialogue techniques

☐ Ensuring that the team meets deadlines for the project

☐ Keeping the library informed on progress and barriers through progress reports

☐ Gathering information and data to make informed decisions

☐ Consulting with the team sponsor and program manager, especially when barriers arise that could result in the project team not meeting the desired outcome of the project

Training for Project Teams to be Successful

There are four additional areas of training that compliment project planning and management training. At UAL we adopted components of the curriculum created by Ingrid Bens (2001), which is supported by an instructor's guide, as well as participant and video guides. The four areas include facilitating effective meetings, gaining commitment and buy-in, effective decision making, and managing group conflict.

FACILITATING EFFECTIVE MEETINGS

Facilitation is an important skill needed for project meetings can be effective. Meetings comprise content and process. It is critical that facilitators are neutral, as team members look to them to provide leadership, although they essentially provide structure and manage the participation or the process. When teams fail, it is often because they do not have a well-defined goal with specific objectives or do not have clear and established agendas. In addition, team members often come unprepared. Facilitators can help ensure that these issues are defined and understood before the start of a project team. Teams often struggle because they have not defined meeting or operating norms, which can lead to problems with time management and decision making. Facilitators can introduce tools and techniques, such as an agenda preparation form, nominal group techniques, or a prioritization matrix that can be used so that team members feel that their ideas are being heard and that time is being used efficiently. The other critical role of a facilitator is to ensure that all assumptions are surfaced and tested. Often discussions go in circles, members argue rather than debating ideas, some staff dominate discussions while others sit passively, and ultimately there is no closure to discussions or agreed-on next steps, which leaves team members feeling ineffective and frustrated. The facilitator needs to listen actively and ask questions for clarity and understanding, as he or she will need to be able to summarize complex ideas in order to achieve shared understanding.

If a given team does not have the luxury to use an outside facilitator, then the project leader will have to balance his or her two distinct roles of chairing and facilitating the meetings. Project leaders are not neutral, in that they have a set of objectives and a timeline by which the objectives must be met, but the role of a facilitator is to foster participation of all team members and allow for time so that the team can reach consensus or collaboration. The project leader can often short-change process and influence decisions, whereas an effective facilitator will control the activities that happen but not the decisions reached. Although it's not ideal to play both the project leader and the facilitator, it can be done as long as the project leader remembers the distinctions between the two roles. Being a facilitative leader is "the act of leading others to participate in what was once the domain of management. It is knowing how to use group processes to maximize participation, productivity, and satisfaction in the workplace. A facilitative leader manages through people, and instead of directing and delegating, facilitators coach and enable others to act efficiently and productively." (Rees, 1991, pp. 2–3)

It is important for both project leaders and facilitators to build in time to assess pulse, process, and pace, as this can keep meetings from going off track. Always end meetings with clear next steps identified, including what will be done, who will do it, and by when. At the beginning of every meeting, you will need to build in time to review these assigned responsibilities to ensure that commitments are being met.

As clarified by Ingrid Bens (2001) and Roger Schwarz (1994), an overview of effective facilitation skills includes the following:

- Clarify the purpose.
- Establish the process and agree on what important words mean.
- Share all relevant information.
- Check for assumptions and inferences.
- Make sure operating norms have been identified and that they are being followed.
- Create buy-in if needed.
- Keep discussions focused and set time frames.
- Stay neutral and objective.
- Keep participants focused on interests, not positions.
- Do not allow participants to take cheap shots or otherwise distract the group.
- Ask participants to explain the reasons behind one's statements, questions, and comments.
- Paraphrase continuously, then invite questions and solutions.
- Act lively and positive.
- Keep participants specific, asking them to use examples.
- Make clear notes.
- Notice when things go wrong.

- Ask good, probing questions.
- Make helpful suggestions.
- Encourage participation and allow members to disagree openly.
- Allow and encourage participants to discuss the discussible issues.
- Design ways to test disagreements and solutions.
- Maintain a good pace.
- Periodically check on how everything is going.
- Move smoothly to new topics.
- Make clear and timely summaries.
- Know when to stop.

Here is an example of what success would look like for participating in a team meeting:

- Review agenda in advance and be prepared for discussion at team meeting.
- During team meeting, clarify understanding of topic.
- Participate in meeting discussions.
- Present alternative viewpoints during meetings using constructive dialogue.
- Volunteer for assigned responsibilities.
- Lead discussion of agenda item, including preparing for agenda item in advance by distributing background information and data to the team before the meeting.
- Rotate recorder responsibility.
- Rotate facilitation responsibility.

GAINING COMMITMENT AND BUY-IN

For teams to be effective, it is important that all members fully participate. In many organizations there are often too many competing priorities and a lack of conviction that teams perform better than individuals. According to Katzenbach and Smith (1993), "Teamwork represents a set of values that encourages behaviors such as listening and constructively responding to points of view expressed by others, giving others the benefit of the doubt, providing support to those who need it, and recognizing the interests and achievements of others. When practiced, such values help all in the organization communicate and work more effectively with one another and, therefore, are good and valuable behaviors." (p. 21)

In addition to helping members of the organization understand the benefits of working in teams, one must also create an environment in which team members can fully participate. In this environment, it is important to ask three critical questions to avoid contributing to low enthusiasm and participation:

1. How will staff find additional time (as staff are already working extra hours) to attend a new set of meetings and the action plans that result from the meetings?
2. Will the organization support the ideas generated by the employees, or will the time spent in meetings be wasted?
3. Will the improvements gained be realized only by the organization and not the individuals involved?

As clarified by Ingrid Bens (2001), to create buy-in, it is important for team members to understand the importance of the work and how it affects them. Questions to ask in order to create buy-in and essentially negotiate participation are the following:

- What is the gain for the organization in solving this problem or fixing this process?
- How will I personally benefit if we solve this problem or fix this process?
- What is blocking me personally from participating? Why might I be reluctant?
- What will it take to overcome these blocks? Under what conditions and with what support will I consider giving this my full attention?

It is important to celebrate when project teams complete their purpose. This is a time to recognize the considerable time and energy that went into the work of the project. It is important to capture what was learned and what could be done differently the next time a team is formed. It is also important for an organization to understand its role in accepting and integrating the work of project teams. Project teams are responsible for handing off new work or changed processes to ongoing work teams in the organization, as it is the nature of ongoing work teams to manage established processes. Project teams will hand off standards in how work should be accomplished and the documentation needed to meet established measures. It is easy for members of the organization who have not participated on a project team or in the decisions made to not own the work of the project team. Project members and administrative leaders in the organization need to play key roles in ensuring that the organization understands the results and benefits of forming teams and that the investment in teams has not been wasted.

EFFECTIVE DECISION MAKING

There are a variety of decision-making options available for organizations, depending on the situation. Understanding which tool to use is a key factor for facilitators (see table 9.1; Bens, 2001). Poor decision making usually occurs when no process or decision-making structure is in place and a facilitator has not been identified. With high emotions and little listening, there is a lack of objective exploration of issues and options, as individuals usually have their minds already made up. Participating in dialogue differs from debating issues to persuade others toward your point of view. Often groups lack complete information when attempting to make decisions, and there is underutilization of the expertise in the organization. Out of sheer frustration, voting is overused. It is critical that the facilitator records decisions and checks to assess people's degree of commitment to the final decision so that individuals can live with the decision once everyone walks out of the room.

Table 9.1: Decision-Making Options

OPTION	PROS	CONS	USE WHEN
Spontaneous agreement	Fast and easy Unites the group	Too fast Lack of discussion	Full discussion not critical Trivial issues
One person decides	Can be fast Clear accountability	Lack of input Low buy-in No synergy	When expertise trumps participation Individual willing to take sole responsibility
Compromise	Encourages discussion Creates a solution	Adversarial Win-lose outcomes divide the group	Positions are polarized and consensus is improbable
Multi-voting	Systematic Objective Participation Feels like a win	Limits dialogue Influenced choices Real priorities may not surface	Sorting or prioritizing a long list of options

Majority voting	Fast Creates high-quality decisions if dialogue precedes voting Clear outcome	May be too fast Winners and losers No dialogue Influenced choices	Issues are trivial There are clear options Division of the group is OK
Consensus building	Collaborative Systematic Participative Discussion oriented Encourages commit- ment	Takes time Requires data and member skills	Issues are important Total buy-in matters Important to think creatively

Working to gain commitment for final decisions can take time, but if well facilitated, it can offer a greater degree of buy-in for those involved. "Creating consensus involves everyone clearly understanding the situation or problem to be decided, analyzing all of the relevant facts together, and then jointly developing solutions that represent the whole group's best thinking about the best outcome for all. It is characterized by a lot of listening, healthy debate, and testing of options. Consensus generates a decision that everyone can live with." (Bens, 2001, p. 33)

Consensus doesn't make everyone happy; rather, the outcome represents the best feasible course of action given the data, information, and circumstances. As the facilitator gains buy-in on the purpose and process, summarizes ideas, ensures that everyone has provided input, and captures input so that individuals can see where and how they have contributed to the discussion; thus, consensus building is done throughout the decision-making process.

MANAGING GROUP CONFLICT

No group can ever become a true team unless it can hold itself and each other accountable. "The problem isn't that teams get into trouble—that's to be expected. The real problem is that team difficulties are too often ignored" (Bens, 2000, p. 1). Effective teams include members with diverse thinking styles, approaches, experience, and knowledge, and they ultimately provide more creativity through different viewpoints. When effective meeting and facilitation processes are not well defined, team members struggle with the differences of opinion in the group: "Conflict can add depth to discussions as members are challenged to elaborate on their ideas so that others better understand them. If everyone already had the same point of view, there would be no need to bring a team together to do the work. When handled well, conflict generated from critically examining ideas is necessary for more effective solutions." (Scholtes, Joiner, & Streibel, 2003, p. 7–1)

At the University of Arizona, all library staff participates in "Constructive Dialogue" training developed by Dances with Opportunity (2002). Early on, when the library formed into teams, Dances with Opportunity (1995) also delivered "Managing Conflict Effectively" training. With this training, skills in constructive dialogue and conflict management are practiced in many ways throughout the organization. Skill development in this area takes time and practice. Initially, the training was designed to support staff in giving constructive feedback during peer development reviews that occur three times a year. This training in constructive dialogue has also been applied when conflict arises between individuals, in project teams, and across library teams. There is an expectation that all members of the organization over time will become skilled at managing conflict. Leaders in the organization are responsible for training, coaching, and mentoring staff to apply constructive dialogue techniques.

For an example of managing group conflict, consider a team member who is having difficulty fully participating in meetings and accomplishing his or her assigned responsibilities and when approached about missing deadlines, responds, "Workload in my team is keeping me from completing assigned tasks." When asked about his or her limited participation in meetings, the individual responds, "Individuals on the project team dominate team meeting and I feel I have little to offer."

In these situations, we apply an effective conflict management technique that includes achieving contact; boiling down the problem; and making choices regarding solutions, agreed-on plans, and next steps. It is important to determine whether the issue is one of can't do or won't do. If it's a can't do, then there is an ability problem with the individual, which can be addressed with a performance plan. If it's a won't do, then there is a motivation problem with the individual, which can be addressed by identifying consequences to behavior. In this example, the project manager or project sponsor (normally a team leader) would consult with the staff member's team leader to engage in a dialogue and assess the workload barrier. If there is a workload issue, the team leader is expected to initiate a plan to remove barrier(s) to ensure that the team member has allocated time to participate fully in the strategic project. As appropriate, other team members of the permanent team may need to be consulted, participate in the discussions, and implement the plan to support their colleague in participating in the team project and balancing the team's work assignments. To address the lack of participation, we would review team member expectations and discuss specifics as to why the team member is not participating. It is important for the individual giving feedback to be direct, specific, and nonpunishing (e.g., "Dan, we agreed to meet at 7:30 a.m., and the past three days you've been late").

In any difficult conversation, it is important for the team leader to follow up on what worked and didn't work, to document next steps, and to track outcomes identified in the agreed-on plan.

Conclusion

It is critical for any organization to assess the environment and enable staff to apply their training and development of their knowledge, skills, and abilities to meet the changing environment of the library and needs of the customer. The outcome of many of our cross-collaborative work and team projects has resulted in many positive outcomes for our faculty, staff, and students at the University of Arizona. The orientation sessions and training programs have enhanced and expanded skill sets for library staff to work collaboratively and respond quickly to strategic opportunities.

REFERENCES

Bens, I. (2001). *Facilitation Dynamics: Interactive Video Series.* Salem, NH: GOAL/QPC.

Brigham Young University Enterprise Project Management Office. (2005). *Project Planning and Management Manual.* Provo, UT: Author.

Dances with Opportunity. (1995). "Managing Conflict Effectively." Tucson, AZ: Author. Retrieved from www.danceswithopportunity.com

Dances with Opportunity. (2002). "Facilitating Constructive Dialogue Workbook." Tucson, AZ: Author. Retrieved from www.danceswithopportunity.com

Katzenbach, J. R., & Smith, D. K. (1993). *The Wisdom of Teams: Creating the High-Performance Organization.* Boston, MA: Harvard Business School Press.

Rees, F. (1991). *How to Lead Work Teams: Facilitation Skills.* San Diego, CA: Pfeiffer.

Scholtes, P. R., Joiner, B. L., & Streibel, B. J. (2003). *The Team Handbook.* Madison, WI: Oriel.

Schwarz, R. M. (1994). *The Skilled Facilitator: Practical Wisdom for Developing Effective Groups.* San Francisco: Jossey-Bass.

University of Arizona Library. (2009). "Fine Arts Center for Creative Photography Planning Project." Retrieved from http://intranet.library.arizona.edu/xf/falccp/docs.html

University of Arizona Library. (2009). "Performance Effectiveness Management System (PEMS). Human Resources & Organizational Effectiveness." Retrieved from http://intranet.library.arizona.edu/teams/hroe/pems/index.html

University of Arizona Library. (2008). "Project, Program & Portfolio Management in the Libraries & CCP." Retrieved from http://intranet.library.arizona.edu/xf/projmanage/index.html

ADDITIONAL RESOURCES

Bens, I. (2000). *Advanced Team Facilitation: Tools to Achieve High Performance Teams*. Salem, NH: GOAL/QPC.

Bens, I. (2008). *Facilitation at a Glance*. Salem, NH: GOAL/QPC.

Brassard, M., & Ritter, D. (1995). *The TEAM Memory Jogger*. Salem, NH: GOAL/QPC.

Brassard, M., & Ritter, D. (1994). *The Memory Jogger II*. Salem, NH: GOAL/QPC.

Gavin, D. A., & Roberto, M. (2005, February). "Change Through Persuasion." *Harvard Business Review, 83*(2), 104–112.

Heinz-Dieter, M., & Kaloyeros, A. E. (2005). "What Campuses Can Do to Pick up the Pace of Decision Making." *Chronicle of Higher Education, 51*(40), B16.

Rees, F. (1998). *The Facilitator Excellence Handbook: Helping People Work Creatively and Productively Together*. San Diego, CA: Jossey-Bass/Pfeiffer.

Yeatts, D. E., & Hyten, C. (1998). *High-Performing Self-Managed Work Teams: A Comparison of Theory to Practice*. Thousand Oaks, CA: Sage.

Steven Carr

chapter 10
Refining the Customer Service Attitude

IN THE THIRD EDITION OF THIS BOOK (AVERY, DAHLIN, & CARVER, 2001), M. Sue Baughman made the case that the development of a customer service attitude was a vital skill for library staff to offer quality service. This concept has resonated with me down each new avenue I have explored as I've updated this chapter. In addition, design professionals tell us that it is imperative to proactively design services to be efficient and to give customers what they want, need, or expect at their first, and at every subsequent, point of contact with the organization. Implementing these design principles requires an even higher level of success in refining the customer service attitude.

In 2007 Arlington County, Virginia, embarked on Arlington CARES, a customer-service initiative designed to be applied to all county departments; Libraries (one of the government departments) was among the early adopters. Arlington also held a management summit with a presentation by Bob O'Neil, president of the International City/County Management Association, featuring interviews with Jim Collins (2005). In both cases, it became apparent that the customer service attitude was a key ingredient to any organization's success. I use each of these programs here to provide a guide and a framework for refining this attitude in your library staff.

Design, design thinking, service design—all are catchphrases in the rapidly evolving field of innovation. Thomas Lockwood (2008), president of the Design Management Institute, has stated, "I've often argued that design has greater potential for impact on the 'triple bottom line' than any other business discipline. So, too, I would argue that service design has greater potential for impact on customer experience than other business techniques" (p. 5).

Like Lockwood, I have experienced these issues as a manager, and I believe his statements to be true. I want to emphasize that hiring people with this attitude is essential. Once they are hired, we need to align staff attitudes toward customer interactions with our principles and the way we design our services. Hence the change in this chapter title from "developing" this customer service attitude to "refining" it; this chapter will show you how to do so.

Much of my interest is centered on the concepts of resource sustainability. As a LEED-accredited professional, I have expertise and certification in the construction and renovation of sustainable facilities. Making facilities green revolves around the use, disposal, and ongoing management of resources and how they are expended. Rarely, however, do these programs look beyond the health and productivity of the people who occupy and work in these buildings. In these economic times during which we struggle daily to maintain our services and collections, I think it is imperative that we also examine the sustainability of the services we offer. Does it really make sense to transfer a $3.95 paperback from one location to another? Can we afford to spend months preparing a public program that has five people in attendance? The definition of sustainability is to use available resources. Reflect for a moment on how often we try to do more with less to maintain customary services without asking this important question: "Do we have enough resources to provide this service?"

It's a common passion among library staff to never want to say no to anyone. Nor do we want to send people away without giving them exactly what they wanted when they came in. However, how do we really know what they wanted? Even in the most basic sense, we cannot say with surety that people coming to the library are looking for books (although that is what the majority of people associate with libraries). Maybe a DVD or the use of a personal computer is what led them to the library. We simply don't know. I maintain that library users exhibit random expectations when they visit. Their expectations are based on whatever their strongest association with a library has been. And this association could be good or bad. If you had a great librarian in school (if your school had a librarian), that could be the basis of your expectation. We simply don't know what someone will expect, nor do we craft any messages to temper those expectations.

Let's look at something most of us are familiar with—the supermarket. If you have lived in the same region of the country for a while, you're probably familiar with the chains that serve your area. What happens when a new chain moves into town? In my region, Wegmans opened a new store. For those of you not familiar, Wegmans is a food lover's paradise. It offers everything from truffles ($499 a pound) to the stuff the other stores carry. When I moved here in 2000, butter at one prominent chain cost $4.95 a pound (store brand). After Wegmans opened, butter dropped to around $2.95. A new supermarket closed because it couldn't stand up to the competition. The other two major chains completely refurbished their stores and lowered their prices.

Why is Wegmans so successful? A number of factors come into play: it offers superb benefits and training to its employees; it covers a variety of customer expectations in one store; and it does everything well. Wegmans has a tremendous number of checkout stations. Lines move swiftly. The managers in charge of the area often open up additional lanes to speed things along. Staff from other parts of the store come up to ring. I have never been there when there have been more than two people in line at a register. When checkers have no one at the register, they step out into the main aisle to welcome shoppers to their lane and alert them that they are available.

Just reflect on the state of the circulation desk at your library for a moment. Are people flocking to self-check? Or do they relish their interactions with your staff? Reflect for a moment on the current state of customer service in your library. Do you feel as if customers are getting more demanding? Are they less understanding? Are they more hurried? Are they not as friendly? What's going on? Aren't we the good guys? Aren't we doing everything and then some to give people what they need? Similarly, reflect on your own behavior as a consumer of services. How do you feel when you go shopping these days? Are you frustrated because you can't find what you want? How about the surly staff in the store? For those of you who love to shop, what makes the experience so meaningful and valuable? I would suggest that just as the expectations of our customers are random and unpredictable, their expectations of staff and services continue to rise.

This leads us to a discussion of touch points. A touch point can be defined as anything that represents your library that a customer or potential customer experiences. Think of touch points as representations of your library's brand.

Your newsletter, street sign, interior colors, building layout, parking situation—these are all touch points. Your library will have hundreds of these. Would you imagine that the typeface of your library sign says a great deal about who you are as a library? It's true. So do your web address, your logo, and the colors used in it. These hundreds of touch points combine to become your customer experience: "The Customer Experience is everything that touches the customer[s] AND their emotional well-being. Touch a customer in a positive emotional manner, and you are likely to have a passionate customer for life. The greater the emotional impact (negative or positive) translates in how passionately your customer commends or scorns you with fellow team members of prospective customers. How your customer feels as a result of engaging you is completely up to you. You are responsible for what happens in your customer relationship." (Rainmaker Group, 2011, n.p.)

I hope you can appreciate the complexity of this idea. Once upon a time, we were able to hire people who liked working with people. We could offer training on how we liked things to be done—the "library way," if you will. Based on our customers and based on the good will that they had for us, this was often a successful formula for good customer service. This paradigm is no longer true in our libraries or, for that matter, even in our own personal lives. This is why it is imperative that we refine our customer service attitude. Because customer perceptions are so complex and essential, managing customer expectations goes well beyond the "did you find what you were looking for today" survey. Every aspect of our library's service program needs to be examined, integrated, and harmonized to be truly effective. Given this concept, customer service is an enterprise-level endeavor. Hence, it needs to be a prominent focus of organizational development in our libraries.

Start Here

The first step in refining your library's customer service attitude starts with your users—both current users and potential users. We need to take a snapshot of what the customers' expectations might be. There are many ways to elicit this information: telephone surveys, in-person surveys outside the library setting, focus groups. Sandra Nelson (2008) outlines one valuable approach. Her work proposes a proven, effective structure with which to organize user data and prioritize library service responses. It also formalizes an approach to gather data from staff and stakeholders.

This feedback is essential but needs further development. Staff can provide and obtain this additional information in a number of ways by looking at additional inputs:

Motivations
- What is motivating customers to use the library?
- What problems are customers experiencing that they are looking for the library to address?
- What suggestions are you receiving from customers for additional or other specialized services?

Meaning
- What compelling users stories have you heard or witnessed?
- Are there common scenarios that can be drawn from the way the library is used?

Modes
- To use the library, what does a customer need to know?
- To use the catalog?
- To use a computer?
- To use the checkout system?

Mapping
- How do customers know where things are?
- Does the mapping language match the terminology the customers use to describe the area?

We also need to learn about the people using or potentially using our libraries. This process will recognize that there are various levels of users, which might include library regulars, library enthusiasts, students, casual users, and users with a native language other than English. Similarly, we need to assess the library staff. What skills do they possess? What about their habits? Also, on the basis of community demographics and our own statistics and or experience, who is not using the library? Let's also assess our facility. How tidy is it? Is it light filled or cluttered? How do customers relate to the space? Remember, we are collecting this information as an assessment, not as a critique of what is wrong with the library. If sustainability is the use of what's available, we need to assess what we have at our disposal as a resource to provide service. We also want to try to bring some clarity to the expectations of customers who we would like to target as potential, highly satisfied library users.

In addition, we need to learn how our services are used. Have you ever followed customers around the building to see what they do? Where do they go first? What next? Try this and record their facial expressions as well as how they move through the facility. It's another way of capturing a snapshot of how users struggle or delight in their use of our services. We can also learn by doing analyses of our workflows. For example:

Outline the steps that you use to obtain materials for the library
- How many people take part in the process?
- How long does it take on average?
- Does your library have an extensive selections process including staff reviews and screening?
- Will you order something a customer requests even if you passed on it during the regular process?

Visit other libraries
- How do they offer services similar to your own?
- What negative and positive reactions do you have to how their services are described and offered?

So far, if you're following along, we have conducted community assessments as prescribed by Nelson (2008). We have also conducted assessments in a more anthropological manner. Now, it would be helpful for staff to compile user stories that capture the results of these steps. The user stories will record the whom, the what, and the why of potential service consumption, as well as identify the many touch points we have in place. User stories would look like this:

> Senior citizens arrived in a van from their assisted living facility. They are coming to the library to return materials they borrowed and borrow some large-type books they haven't read before.
>
> A four-year-old's caregiver brings the child to the library for a story hour.
>
> A new resident comes to the library looking for information about the community.
>
> A regular user comes to the desk looking for a book that just came in; she was looking at the catalog and noted it was received yesterday.

A resident clicks on the library link from the town's website. He is interested in learning where the library is and the services that it provides.

You have now compiled the raw data necessary to analyze the services you provide or would need to provide to satisfy these user stories. Look at the first user story. Here's how it could be useful:

Senior citizens: Identifies potential or current user

Arrived in a van: Do we have a spot for vans to drop customers off safely? Is it so identified?

From their assisted living facility: How many users are there at this facility? Is it more economical for us to go there? Can someone with limited mobility use the library effectively?

To return materials: Can senior citizens do this easily? Is it clear where to go? Do they need to do anything else to return successfully? Do we need to check things in so more may be borrowed?

Borrow large type: Do we have this type of collection? How current and useful is it?

They haven't read before: Is there a way to track what they've read? Could we prepare materials for pickup? How could this be accomplished? Do other groups need this service? What about reader's advisory?

As you can see, a list of questions emerges from this analysis. Common service needs are identified. A prioritized list of services can be developed using this technique.

Once this list of services has been compiled, a comparison to existing services can begin. Do we do things that have not been identified on the list? If so, why? Do these unidentified services support those identified in our user stories? If they don't, we might have uncovered an excellent service that is irrelevant in today's climate. To cite an earlier example, if we are spending hours reviewing book reviews before buying materials, might not our vendor perform this service for us? Especially if none of our customer stories mention reviewed or screened materials being of value. Might we not rethink our staff usage in this regard? It is only in identifying processes and services that we can give up that we can free up staff to provide processes and services that customers are actually looking for.

Now that you have identified the services you are able to provide given the resources you have, we can move on. The final step in refining your library's customer service attitude is to define it. This is where a process such as Arlington CARES can be helpful. In a series of staff meetings throughout the library system, discussions were held to see what skills staff thought were essential in supporting the services identified earlier on. It is critical that the staff decide (with input from administrators) what is essential. If this list diverges greatly from the vision of the library's administration, you will have identified a training gap for staff development experts to address.

In our case, we identified the ways in which we wanted to interact with our customers. What would we feel illustrated a successful staff interaction with a customer at different places around the library system? We were further challenged that the quality of these interactions had to be quantifiable. How would we measure success? The results are recorded in the following sections.

Arlington CARES Standards

TAILORED AND CONSOLIDATED FOR THE LIBRARY DEPARTMENT, OCTOBER 2007

All standards apply to internal and external customers.

C—Communication

1. Use standard interview questions with each customer. See below for "standard" opening and closing questions; content of other questions will vary with answers from the customer.

   - Opening question: "How may I help you?" or "Do you need some help?"
   - Closing question: "Do you need help with anything else today?"
   - Success measured by
     - Staff and supervisor observation
     - Surveys and other patron checklists
     - Secret shopper

2. Recognize individual customer priorities and provide effective service that is obvious to all.

   - Staff at all locations are trained to assist at busy desks; customers are aware that extra staff has been called to assist.

- Facilitate customer referrals by calling first, accompanying patron, and providing background information to next service provider.
- Maximize use of all public service stations with better signage and maximum staffing.
- Success measured by
    - New, improved signage
    - Surveys and other patron checklists
    - Staff feedback about phoning ahead
    - Staff and supervisor observation

A—Awareness

1. Be knowledgeable of the work and services provided by different library divisions and units.

    - Once per year and as needed, staff reviews the Library Online Orientation and correctly directs patrons applying module content.
    - Managers summarize and communicate important information and news daily to employees on all shifts.
    - Success measured by
        - Employees being able to answer most questions at their location
        - Staff and supervisor observation
        - Staff feedback
        - Informal patron feedback

2. Keep current in your knowledge of library and county events, structure, and services.

    - Review Squirrel (the library intranet) at least once daily, and review the library home page, the county home page, and AC Source (the county's intranet) at least twice a week.
    - Success measured by
        - Employees being able to answer most questions at their location
        - Supervisor observation
        - Staff feedback
        - Informal patron feedback

R—Respect

1. Demonstrate the following behavior in each customer interaction:

    - We will start with . . .
        - Making eye contact
        - Greeting warmly

- Creating an atmosphere conducive to a positive exchange
- Giving full attention throughout the interaction

  - We will continue with . . .
    - Validating the person
    - Providing correct information
    - Honoring their time (recognizing different needs)
    - Maintaining objectivity
    - Recognizing diversity
    - Maintaining confidentiality

  - We will conclude the transaction with . . .
    - Making any appropriate referral(s)
    - Offering any value-added information
    - Asking if we have met their needs
    - Thanking them
    - Inviting them back

  - Success measured by . . .
    - Staff and supervisor observation
    - Use of compliment cards
    - Results from surveys
    - Ratings from electronic transactions
    - Kudos
    - Secret shopper

E—Execution

1. Deliver timely, reliable, high-quality services to all customers.

   - Employees meet standards of important processes, as defined by their unit and/or division (standards for success defined by each unit as part of the process).
   - Create and utilize opportunities to provide "WOW" service experiences for library patrons and opportunities for staff to share WOW customer service transactions.
   - Success measured by
     - Staff-reported instances of WOW service (WOW Forum)
     - Staff and supervisor observation
     - Customer feedback from surveys, secret shopper, and so on

As you can see, we identified communication as the most important skill that we needed to possess. This was a skill directed at internal and external customer alike. Next was awareness of what we were doing as a library system and where we were going. We noted that most of our issues with customers and staff involved a perceived lack of respect, so we highlighted this. Last on our list was how well the job we were doing was executed. It was last on the list because we concluded that one could be excellent at one's job but, lacking communication or respect, would ultimately be unsuccessful.

Let's outline the steps again:

Identify all points at which customers (current and potential) touch the library.
- Consider how others use information you provide.
- Consider places you might like to reach out to potential customers.
- What are the elements of these interactions?

Look at staff strengths and passions.
- Information, customer service, reading, seniors, serving children?
- What kinds of people make up the staff?
- How do they relate to the others that they work with?

Define what's important—what statements do you want to make with each touch point you provide?
- Ask customers.
- Ask your governing body.
- What are your essential beliefs about what the library does?

Consensus build—what can you agree on?
- Agree to disagree.
- Publish your results—widely.

Look at other organizations for great interactions and partnerships.
- What do you identify with?
- What kind of interactions do you like? Why?

Lose the attitude that everything must be perfect right from the start and at every moment.
- Loosen up.
- Give people permission to fail or to succeed.

Identify irrelevant services or processes and give them up.
- Grieve the loss of things that people liked to do that aren't needed anymore.
- Celebrate the past success of products no longer useful.

Model your vision.
- Discuss why others' needs are different and why they are important.
- Discuss differences openly.
- Don't play favorites.
- Be visible and talk to people.

Identify effective measurements and assessments.
- What will define success?
- What criteria will we use to decide whether to continue?

Evaluate staff in a positive way toward successful behaviors and outcomes.
- Connect staff with what they enjoy about their work.
- Connect staff with customer feedback.

Celebrate success and laugh at less-than-success.
- Reward success and failure.
- Never stop evaluating or refining.

Conclusion

Change isn't easy. In tough economic times, we are faced with tough choices to make from sometimes-unattractive alternatives. Only by aligning our currently available resources (e.g., staff, time, dollars, facilities, technologies) with our service priorities can we truly offer effective services that our communities need and want. The successful customer service attitude reflects this understanding. Good customer service is only available from a staff that is not overextended, not undertrained, or not engaged in the mission and service philosophy of the library. Staff inclusion and participation is essential to refining the customer service attitude. I hope the steps and concepts outlined here present a vision for this process and compel you to try it.

REFERENCES

Avery, E. F., Dahlin, T., & Carver, D. A. (Eds.) & Library Administration and Management Association Staff Development Committee. (2001). *Staff Development: A Practical Guide* (3rd ed.). Chicago, IL: American Library Association.

Collins, J. C. (2005). *Good to Great: Why Some Companies Make the Leap—and Others Don't.* Boulder, CO: J. Collins.

Lockwood, T. (2008, Winter). "Design for the Service Industry is the Design of Our Entire Experience." *Design Management Review*, 5.

Nelson, S. (2008). *Strategic Planning for Results.* Chicago, IL: American Library Association.

Rainmaker Group. (2011). "Improve Customer Experiences with Touchpoint Development." Retrieved from www.therainmakergroupinc.com/add.asp?ID=13

Maureen Sullivan

chapter 11 / # Leading from Any Position

I N TODAY'S LIBRARY WORKPLACE THERE IS A GREAT NEED FOR CON-
tinuous improvement and innovation. Staff at all levels experience
changes in the work they perform and the services they provide on
a regular basis. Gone is the time when the planning and execution of
these changes could be done effectively and in a timely way by managers and supervisors. Libraries deliver their best performance when
every staff member contributes her or his best work. Competent and
committed staff members contribute their best ideas and work with colleagues
to adapt procedures, programs, and practices to ensure the best service to the
communities they serve. This requires a mind-set on the part of everyone, especially individual staff, that everyone is a leader and that each person can lead
from where he or she is. This approach assumes a set of principles:

> Regardless of position title or classification, years of experience, role, or
> work area, every person on the staff has opportunities to lead, show
> initiative, and enable others to contribute ideas and work of value to
> the library.
> The library is an inclusive workplace in which everyone's ideas, perspec-
> tives, and approaches have value. The diversity of these among staff
> enriches the set of options and the possibility for effective and suc-
> cessful outcomes.

There is mutual responsibility for the success of projects, the work of each unit, and the overall performance of the library.

Real collaboration requires an appreciation of different areas of competence and a commitment to take advantage of complementary strengths and abilities.

The library is a workplace and a laboratory for learning and development. Every experience is an opportunity for growth and competency development. Often the most complex and challenging situations offer the greatest means for development of leadership competence.

Leadership, talent development, and organizational performance thrive in organizations that practice appreciative inquiry, those that assume an organization "is a mystery to be embraced," and not "a problem to be solved" (Hammond, 1998, p. 24).

When the organization's culture and formal leadership value and expect leadership from everyone, staff perform accordingly.

The library director, the human resources director, and the senior leadership team must take the lead to create a work environment that will enable informal, shared leadership to flourish throughout the library. Some steps to take include the following:

1. Assess the library's current state of readiness.
    - Focus on identification of current strengths—what now exists that will be a foundation for moving forward.
    - Report the results.
    - Learn from them.

2. Create a vision of the future desired workplace.
    - Involve as many staff as possible at all levels.
    - Focus on the future and possibilities.
    - Make the experience fun.
    - Map the big picture.

3. Be optimistic and promote the positive.
    - Appreciate each person and his or her contribution.
    - Treat everyone with respect.
    - Identify examples that have already occurred; tell those stories.

4. Gain the commitment of the leadership team.
   - Spend time in discussion of what it will mean to have a library that values leading from any position.
   - Expect their commitment, support, and leadership.
   - Identify any barriers or concerns.
   - Coach and provide immediate feedback.

5. Make the workplace safe for open and honest communication.
   - Build trust.
   - Encourage open expression of all ideas.
   - Engage in dialogue.
   - Reduce defensiveness.
   - Appreciate expressions of skepticism.

6. Reward risk taking.
   - Encourage staff to experiment.
   - Appreciate effort.
   - Explain that mistakes are part of the experience and are opportunities for learning.
   - Promote pilot projects and moderate risks.
   - Provide the resources and time needed.

7. Help staff become resources for one another.
   - Create structures (e.g., task forces, open forums) to encourage people to get together to share experiences and ideas.
   - Deal with disagreements and conflicts in constructive ways.
   - Implement a peer-coaching program.
   - Create learning partnerships.

8. Ensure that everyone learns about leadership.
   - Learn about current theories of effective leadership.
   - Invite staff to identify what effective leadership means and looks like to them.
   - Identify norms and practices that will support informal leadership in the library.
   - Develop a statement of the library's philosophy about leadership and best practices for everyone to follow.

9. Analyze the current systems in the library (e.g., resource allocation, policy development, communication, decision making, performance feedback, training and development, work design, technology).
    - Make changes to ensure that the systems are connected and aligned.
    - Ensure that there are feedback loops.
    - Publish information about the systems—their purpose and rules to follow.

10. Affirm the importance of people.
    - Expect their commitment and positive contributions.
    - Listen and respond to their questions.
    - Ask each person to create her or his own learning and development plan.
    - Express appreciation for each person's current contribution.
    - Convey the importance of everyone's continued contribution.

Key Competencies for Leading from Any Position

The following are key competencies for leading from any position:

Foresight, the ability to envision the future and to think for the long term as well as the present and the short term.

The ability to imagine new realities and to share them with colleagues to develop a shared vision of the future.

A strong commitment to high-quality customer-centered service and to continuous improvement.

An ability to anticipate the consequences of action and to assess the risks in decision making.

Actively seeking out information from a variety of sources in the library, in the community, and beyond.

Strong interpersonal skills, trustworthiness, and the ability to establish and maintain working relationships based on trust and mutual respect.

Commitment to the library's values and the ability to behave in ways that are congruent with personal values and the espoused values of the library.

A willingness to challenge behavior that is inconsistent with organizational values, norms, and expectations; skills to give constructive feedback to others.

An understanding of the political environment, both in the library and externally.

The ability to influence and persuade others.

Appreciating others for who they are, valuing differences, and promoting diversity and inclusion among the staff.

Accurate self-awareness and knowledge, and the willingness to act on that self-awareness and knowledge.

Deep commitment to contributing one's personal best and working with colleagues in support of their efforts to do so.

Ability to manage oneself and assume self-responsibility to be accountable for contributions and high performance on a continuing basis.

The research on how competent leaders develop tells us that the most effective way to develop leadership competence is through trial and error on the job. This action-learning approach requires that the learner

- Knows the competencies for effective leadership
- Has a clear understanding of his or her current capabilities and strengths
- Clarifies the areas for development and sets goals for development
- Makes a firm commitment to achieve the development goals
- Has ample opportunities to practice the competencies over an extended period of time, usually six to eighteen months
- Has a supportive work environment
- Receives challenging assignments and carries them out under the general guidance of an experienced and competent leader or manager

- Gets regular and targeted feedback on performance
- Engages in continual self-reflection and self-awareness

Leading from Any Position: Tools for Planning

One simple approach to start to increase one's self-awareness and self-knowledge is the following template for planning leadership development, which can be used by individuals, teams, and organizations.

LEADERSHIP DEVELOPMENT: SELF-ASSESSMENT AND PLANNING

My strengths in the area of leadership include: _____

_____

To be more effective, I need to work on: _____

_____

Review these areas for improvement and develop a goal for each. Add as many goal-planning areas as needed.

Goal: _____

A starting point is: _____

Resources I'll need include: _____

Steps I can take within the next two months: _____

I'll know I've been successful when: _____

As I work on my development, I am likely to face barriers such as: _____

_____

I can seek support from: _____

LEADERSHIP DEVELOPMENT: CREATING A PERSONAL VISION

Think ahead to five years from now.

- Where will you be?
- What will you be doing?
- With whom will you be?
- What will your work be?
- What will your life be?
- How do you hope others will describe you?

REFERENCE

Hammond, S. A. (1998). *The Thin Book of Appreciative Inquiry* (2nd ed.). Plano, TX: Thin Book Publishing Company.

ADDITIONAL RESOURCES

Bennis, W. (2009). *On Becoming a Leader* (4th ed.). New York, NY: Basic Books.

Bennis, W., & Goldsmith, J. (2010). *Learning to Lead: A Workbook on Becoming a Leader* (4th ed.). New York, NY: Basic Books.

Goleman, D., Boyatzis, R. Z., & McKee, A. (2004). *Primal Leadership: Learning to Lead with Emotional Intelligence*. Boston, MA: Harvard Business Press.

Seifter, H., & Economy, P. (2001). *Leadership Ensemble: Lessons in Collaborative Management from the World's Only Conductorless Orchestra*. New York, NY: Henry Holt.

Maureen Sullivan

chapter 12

Developing Bench Strength

Succession Planning

L IBRARIES TODAY FACE MANY CHALLENGES, A NUMBER OF WHICH are complex and represent situations not faced previously. The key to ensuring that libraries can meet these challenges is to have a staff that is ready and able to solve complex problems, to develop innovative solutions, and to continue to develop the intellectual capacity needed to keep pace in the increasingly digital and physical context. It is critically important to recognize that the only renewable resource in any library organization is the intellectual capacity of its staff. A key strategy must be to create a workplace that promotes retention and ensures ongoing development of the competencies staff at all levels will need to perform effectively in the ever-changing context in which they exist.

Among the steps that managerial leaders can take to accomplish this are:

Focus on staff development as a key initiative in the library. Make it a clear priority.

Connect and align the staff development program with the larger change initiatives in the library.

Take a broad view of who will have the talent and commitment to grow and develop as the organization evolves. Be careful not to prejudge potential too early.

Create opportunities for new staff to interact with effective, more experienced staff and to learn from them.

Identify meaningful projects and assignments that will challenge and stretch potential staff throughout the library.

Ensure that managerial leaders in the library are held accountable for effective leadership. Insist that their leadership practice matches the espoused leadership philosophy and values of the library.

Remain alert to complex and challenging situations. Put managers and potential leaders in those situations.

Make your staff development program one that is based on an action-learning model.

Establish a mentoring program. Encourage broad engagement and participation in the program.

Create a learning culture in the library.

Strengthen Leadership Capacity Throughout the Library: A Tool for Leaders

Noel Tichy is known for his approach to leadership development, what he has called the teachable point of view. He postulates that the most powerful learning experiences in leadership development occur when leaders teach their own points of view to others by communicating their ideas, values, concerns, and issues. This approach asks leaders to do two things: to develop their own teachable point of view (i.e., their perspective of what it takes to be successful in their organization and what it takes to lead others) and to create a dynamic story to convey this. Although this tool is especially appropriate for managerial leaders, any other staff members can also use it effectively.

The first step, preparing to develop one's teachable point of view, begins with a set of questions for reflection in each of the four major components: ideas, values, edge, and emotional energy. The second step calls for the development of the teachable point of view, and the third step is the one in which the individual formulates the story to be told.

STEP 1: THE LEADER'S IDEAS, VALUES, EDGE, AND EMOTIONAL ENERGY

Ideas

> What are your ideas about the future for libraries? For your library?
>
> What will make the library successful?
>
> What does the library do to create value for its constituents?
>
> What might it do?

Values

> What are the values of your library—the ones the library lives by?
>
> How do these values support the library's work to create value for its constituents?
>
> Are any of these values likely to impede future efforts to create value for the library's constituents?

Edge (An Unflinching Readiness to Face Reality and the Courage to Act)

> What tough issues are you dealing with? What are the critical decisions you face?
>
> What holds you back?
>
> What might be the consequences of delayed decision making?

Emotional Energy

> What do you do to keep yourself energized?
>
> What do you do to motivate others?

STEP 2: DEVELOPING A TEACHABLE POINT OF VIEW

Reflect on your responses to the previous set of questions and reply to the following:

> What does it take to be successful in your leadership practice?
>
> What is required to motivate and lead others?

STEP 3: YOUR LEADERSHIP STORY

Develop your story around these three elements:

> The case for change—why things cannot continue as they are.
>
> Where we are going—the picture of a better future.
>
> How we will get there—what we will have to do, stop doing, or do differently to create a better future.

Succession Management: Key Criteria for an Effective Program

Succession management is a deliberate and systematic effort by an organization to develop and prepare people to assume leadership positions and other roles of greater responsibility. It is a proactive approach that ensures continuity in key positions by cultivating talent from within the organization through planned development activities. The conditions for a successful program include the following:

Staff members have opportunities to pursue and learn from new challenges.

Managerial leaders believe in the potential of people to contribute beyond their current performance levels. They expect staff to grow and develop.

There is a clear and aspirational vision for the future of the organization. This vision inspires staff to contribute their best performance.

There is a systematic approach to identifying and nurturing talent.

Career paths, rather than career ladders, are available.

There is a diverse workforce, and diversity is valued.

There is an open flow of information across the organization.

Staff are recognized and appreciated for their achievements and contributions.

Learning and development plans spell out performance goals and identify areas for competency development.

Staff receive regular, specific, and timely feedback on their performance. Managerial leaders provide positive reinforcement on an ongoing basis.

There is an explicit commitment to a broad and inclusive approach to succession management.

Senior leadership continually affirm their commitment to staff development and to the succession management program.

A Model for Creating a Succession Management Program

There are two key phases: preparation and talent development.

PHASE 1: PREPARATION

Determine future needs and identify key positions and areas of work activity.

Determine the competencies that will be needed to perform this work.

Identify potential talent in the organization.

Engage supervisors and managers in talent review meetings. The outcome of such meetings is agreement on a list of "potentials."

PHASE 2: TALENT DEVELOPMENT

Determine how competencies will be developed and prepare an overall plan.

For each individual, determine where competency development is needed. Focus on enhancing strengths and addressing any areas of weakness.

Develop performance goals.

Engage each person in the preparation of a development plan.

Identify the development opportunities that are available in the organization.

Provide coaching and mentoring on a regular basis.

Retaining Staff

A critical element in ensuring bench strength is the retention of the high-performing, talented staff. This requires the creation of a work environment in which staff can achieve high degrees of work satisfaction, accomplish work that is meaningful and rewarding, and develop colleague relationships that contribute to professional development and personal mastery.

Some steps and guidelines are the following:

1. Identify the staff you want to retain. Focus on those individuals. Managers and administrators often give more attention to the problem performers than to the best performers.
2. Be sure they know you want to retain them.
3. Learn what their sources of job satisfaction are. Find out what most motivates them to achieve their best performance.
4. Recognize their accomplishments and do so in ways that are meaningful to them.
5. Stop by their work areas to thank them for their contributions.
6. Seek their input on what the library can do to improve service.
7. Involve them in planning for major change, new projects, and so on.
8. Invite them to identify challenging new assignments.
9. Do whatever you can to ensure that their compensation reflects a recognition of their contributions.

10. Move beyond specific position descriptions and develop a more fluid approach to work assignments. Invite staff to create their own work portfolios.

11. Take time to educate staff about the profession, the parent organization, and the business we are in.

12. Follow the platinum rule: treat others as they want to be treated.

13. Encourage staff to freely express their ideas and listen to those ideas with an open mind.

14. Build a climate of trust in each relationship and in the organization.

15. Establish a mentoring program. Assign each new staff member a buddy, someone who will introduce him or her to the organization and its culture right away. Create opportunities for multiple mentors. Select the mentors carefully and prepare them for this role. Be clear about expectations.

16. Know everyone on the staff. Know their names and the work they do.

17. Clearly communicate performance expectations and standards.

18. Be sure that your orientation program is thorough and includes an emphasis on getting to know the culture, norms, and practices of the organization.

19. Establish a mentoring program that is flexible to meet each individual's needs and preferences. Include opportunities for multiple mentors.

20. Implement an individual learning and development planning process. Provide resources and support to help staff pursue their goals.

21. Find out what staff think helps them in their work and what hinders them from doing their best. Take steps to remove the hindrances.

22. Hold managers accountable for the coaching and development of staff.

23. Expect managers to take an active interest in staff development and to spend time with each staff member on a regular basis. Make this an explicit performance expectation.

24. Schedule social events to enable staff to get to know each other across the organization. This creates the opportunity to form a network of relationships and a community in the organization.

ADDITIONAL RESOURCES

Cohen, E., & Tichy, N. (1997, May). "How Leaders Develop Leaders." *Training and Development*. Retrieved from www.noeltichy.com/HowLeadersDevelop Leaders.pdf

Conger, J., & Fulmer, R. M. (2003, December). "Developing Your Leadership Pipeline." *Harvard Business Review*, 76–84.

Fulmer, R. M., & Conger, J. A. (2004). *Growing Your Company's Leaders: How Great Organizations Use Succession Management to Sustain Competitive Advantage.* New York, NY: AMACOM.

Schmidt, M., & Schmidt, C. (2010, May). "How to Keep Your Top Talent." *Harvard Business Review*, 54–61.

Wiseman, L., & McKeown, G. (2010, May). "Bringing Out the Best in Your People." *Harvard Business Review*, 117–121.

Part III

Tackling Change Through Training

Julie Todaro

chapter 13

Planning a Training and Development Infrastructure for Library and Information Environments

Roles and Responsibilities

O F THE MANY PLANS NECESSARY FOR LIBRARIES TODAY, THE training and development plan may be the most important and—odds are—if you are reading this guide, you don't need to be convinced that an organized approach to training and development is critical to the success of the employees and the success of the organization and ultimately to the success of the patron, client, or customer. What most managers need, however, includes an assessment of the recent past and current state of learning in libraries, rationales for a new approach to learning to articulate support for administrative commitment, roles and responsibilities for training, and examples of learning infrastructures for all types and sizes of libraries.

An Assessment of the Recent Past and Current State of Learning in Libraries

A simple question-and-answer assessment of organizations can determine how learning occurs in today's workplace. Although there is one set of answers and no simple score to determine a need for change, these questions are designed to make managers think—and specifically to rethink workplace learning and create a plan for change:

- Do you have random training opportunities for staff or a specific plan for learning for each employee?
- Have you articulated the differences between and among the concepts of orientation, training, development, and education?
- Do you have an annual plan for learning for the organization overall, or have you looked ahead two to three years to anticipate employee and organizational needs?
- Does your organization typically train staff at random locations, or have you designated learning workstations and specific environments for learning?
- Do you and your employees schedule learning activities for a variety of times throughout the workweek and month, or do you have self-directed, standardized, and scheduled learning times?
- Have you identified core and specialized competencies needed and required for ongoing learning?
- Do you only have one type of learning for your employees such as individual, small group, or larger group, or have you identified specific self-directed, team, or partnership and cooperative learning?
- Typically, outcomes, goals, and objectives of an organization have had little written, specific commitment to teaching and learning. Has your organization identified and added to policies, procedures, and all documents of the organization? Do your individual employees have learning plans?
- Budgeting for training has typically been discussed primarily under "travel account" categories, with limited definitions and guidelines. Do you have all learning monies in one account or divided into specific learning activities?
- Methods of choosing trainers, methods of training, and matching training needs and curriculum to staff learning styles is recommended for work environments. Do you identify learning roles and responsibilities for employees? Do you match employees to their teaching and learning styles and preferences?

RATIONALES FOR A NEW APPROACH

Libraries have been experiencing and will continue to experience dramatic changes in organizations. The need for ongoing orienting, training, developing, and educating of employees—or continuous learning—for all aspects of management and public and technical services is becoming of paramount importance. Specifically:

- Selection, investment in, and designation of institutional trainers is critical.
- Systems for communicating basic and changing information on continuous learning activities are needed.
- There is a need to integrate learning and learning for work success as a specific, measured part of job descriptions, expectations for performance, and evaluation.
- Managers need to consider including a competitive process for assigning or awarding monies not for orientation and training but for development and education opportunities for staff rather than the more typical noncompetitive distribution of funding (e.g., employees bid on any available development or travel dollars by submitting their needs and what venues meet those needs and how they will repurpose the information upon return to the organization).
- Managers need to explore alternative learning opportunities strategies (e.g., remote, distance or desktop, and train-the-trainer assignments).
- Managers should consider designating learning stations in libraries designed for self-directed training, development, and education as "staff only" for permanent, temporary, or shared (patron in the morning and staff in the afternoon) focus.
- Managers should consider increased placement of training in service and in product vendor contracts.
- Nonacademic training is becoming more available and acceptable. *Nonacademic* is defined as not in the classroom or not connected with higher education. This could be vendor or umbrella institution training, such as city or county or business such as hospital.
- Librarians should create a hue and cry for improved self-directed or group product training from vendors including improved (or any!) user instruction information with products.
- Managers should build a holistic learning budget, pulling from travel and training support accounts.
- Librarians and managers should consider moving to additional or alternative means of evaluation mechanisms in which train-

ing and performance related to learning is specifically assessed (e.g., using self-assessments that include evaluation forms or portfolios).

- Managers should continue to focus on collaborative and partnership learning opportunities in umbrella organizations, with area libraries and nonprofit organizations, with regional or state organizations, through associations, and among types of libraries.
- The focus for learning should include using active learning techniques.
- The focus for learning should be at point-of-use environments and should include teaching at work desks or public service workstations.
- Orientation, training, development, and education must be matched to staff learning styles and needs.

ROLES AND RESPONSIBILITIES FOR TRAINING

Each Staff Member Is Responsible for His or Her Own Training

Managers must first believe and then articulate their belief and their expectation for each and every employee to be responsible for full participation in their own basic work orientation and training and to be committed to and active in continuous training as well as proactive in group and self-identification of training needs. Ultimately, employees must understand that they are responsible for many aspects of the training process and that management expectation is that they must embrace—in an ongoing process—their own role and responsibilities in receiving and participating in training in the organization. In order to ensure that all employees fully participate in the process then, managers should:

- Include the importance of each employee's continuous learning and training plan in the management expectation statement
- Build individual training roles and responsibilities into every job description with matching terminology in employee evaluations
- Include—in all interview question sets—a statement on and questions relating to continuous learning requirements for all jobs as well as each individuals' role in and responsibility for their own training

- Provide avenues and pathways for employees to assess competency levels
- Provide avenues and pathways for employees to assess learning styles and learning interest levels
- Integrate competency growth and training plans into each employee's work plan

Ensuring these elements are present in the organization readies employees in the organization for a continuous learning work setting.

Each Staff Member Is Responsible for Participation in Continuous Learning for Others

In management expectation statements and in continuous learning and training-plan discussions, managers must identify each employee's role and responsibility in other employees' continuous learning and training. This includes the following:

- The importance of each employee's participation in the organization's orientation program for others, such as new employees and other employees in cross-training programs
- A statement on each employee's responsibility to keep any processes and practices up to date for providing accurate orientation and training materials for others
- Statements in the job description with matching terminology in employee evaluations regarding employee roles and responsibilities for others in the organization, such as the importance of working in teams and the importance of relationships with coworkers in other departments and locations
- A statement on and questions relating to working with others and working on teams in all interview question sets
- Avenues and pathways for employees to team with other individuals with similar learning styles or levels for peer-training or teaching

There Is No Trainer, and the Manager Must Assume Management of Training, Development, and Education Roles and Responsibilities

Given not only the size and type of organization but also existing budget and budget priorities, it is highly likely that managers or a manager must assume all orientation, training, development, and education roles and responsibilities. If this is the case, managers should strive to articulate each employee's roles and responsibilities as outlined earlier but should also provide an extensive continuous learning infrastructure that stands on its own. The infrastructure for orientation should include print or online and web content for the following:

- A workplace, environment, or location tour—primary and secondary areas, safety issues for individual employees, comfort, key people, and so on
- Administrative issues—paperwork, insurance, benefits, and emergency management concerns
- Organizational policies and management documents—mission and values, outcomes measured, and customer issues
- Office policies and procedures the employee will be required to know and use in the first few weeks and months of work
- Basic job and position information—the job description, performance assessment and evaluation, reporting documents, and workplace calendars
- Personnel and human resources—organizational guidelines and rules, and behavioral expectations
- Workplace tools—management information systems, documentation, and learning information
- Critical client, customer, or patron profile introductory information and customer service policies and procedures

The infrastructure for training—with the focus on competencies, specifically skills and abilities—should include print or online and web content for the following:

- First-year, job-specific content that is typically more standardized to employees across work groups and departments and covers the basic competencies and skills sets needed to perform basic job functions in the organization
- Training divided into basic, intermediate, and advanced levels that employees need to perform their basic job and to grow in their job, and to adjust to what's new and what is coming in the near future
- Training for employees to learn about other employee roles and responsibilities that overlap or intersect with their own work

The infrastructure for development—often referred to as professional development—focuses on content for employee learning that

- Addresses a change in attitude or values
- Moves beyond basic job functions
- Includes expansion of roles and responsibilities
- Addresses new responsibilities
- Dictates different ways of presenting content or teaching (e.g., cases, scenarios)
- Dictates different ways for employees to learn (e.g., prior study) and interactive exercises, expert presentation, and short-term or ongoing discussion between and among employees and between employees and management
- The infrastructure for education for employees focuses on the need for an employee to have a change in knowledge. Employee education typically is characterized by the following:
  Provides more in-depth content
  Typically covers longer periods of time for learning
  Includes more advanced activities
  Is thought to be "harder"
  Can involve testing for mastery before completion
  Often dictates—as does development—different teaching or learning pedagogy

Learning Infrastructures

Once managers have articulated the training roles and responsibilities of individual employees, there are a number of different approaches to establishing infrastructures for providing learning opportunities in organizations. Some libraries focus on an infrastructure using internal opportunities, whereas others plan infrastructures with external opportunities. Although a classic plan for infrastructure would include establishing a training department in the library and the budgeting and hiring of one or more individuals whose jobs would cover all learning needs, most libraries can't afford that approach.

INTERNAL OPPORTUNITIES
Internal designations of roles and responsibilities can include determining employees who would be considered resident experts, training specialists, edu-

cation counselors, mentors, and coaches. These can include both full-time and part-time commitments. Some of the steps that managers should take to decide on the level of commitment are analyzing an organization's needs and staffing realities such as competency levels, potential, and interests, as well as analyzing or revising job descriptions and balancing job responsibilities, rather than just adding on new responsibilities, and revising or developing job ads that outline and ask employees to apply for positions. Although there are a variety of definitions out there, the following sections cover descriptions for these individuals.

Resident Experts

Resident experts are employees who have been identified as knowledgeable or potentially knowledgeable in an area. They may have content background that is unique. They do not teach, present, or give workshops; instead, they are on call to answer questions, give advice, or perform support activities such as installation or troubleshooting. Besides being on call, they might have in-person or online office hours and standardized forms for reporting needs. They might also design and maintain learning wikis or blogs, or sponsor bulletin boards or online lists. In conjunction with instruction design or support people, they produce tip sheets, simple instructions, or curricula to maximize their knowledge. Furthermore, resident experts may provide managers with evaluative data on employee training plans if working with employees has been assigned or tied to an employee's performance conditions. Much of the work and discussion can be done virtually or digitally.

Training Specialists

Specialist employee positions typically have all or a major part of their job designated for the design and delivery of teaching and learning activities. They teach, train, educate, develop, plan, coordinate, and present information, as well as assess, track, measure, report on, and communicate the learning activities of the organization. They can be assigned to work with resident experts, online content designers (or they may design curriculum themselves), and other content specialists on curricula. Specialists provide avenues for staff input, and they may have background or experience in teaching or learning (education) or communication and presentation skills. Specialists may also be asked to provide evaluative data on training plans for managers. Although much of the work can be done virtually or digitally, specialists must be able to determine the best mode or method for connecting with an employee—although they might do it virtually or digitally, it is also often done face-to-face or in person.

Training and Learning Council or Staff Development Council

Councils are advisory bodies to training programs for employees. They request, maintain, and review data; advise managers on assessment and direction; assist in evaluation of the commercial curriculum; identify curricula that need to be produced internally; and project future trends. The majority of council members, however, do not design curricula or deliver training activities. Much of the work and discussion can be done virtually or digitally.

Staff Development and Learning Committees or Teams

Committees or teams are work groups designed to aid in designing and maintaining the learning activities of the organization. If there is only a committee or team and no council, then the committee or team may perform some duties of the council outlined in the previous section, but they are primarily work support for training staff. These groups, obviously, would exist in environments where there are not large numbers of employees or employees whose primary responsibility is training. Staff development and learning committees or teams are involved in employee evaluation only to the extent that these groups design the evaluation process and gather and present evaluation data, typically in the aggregate. Much of the work and discussion can be done virtually or digitally.

Train-the-Trainers

Although typically considered a process instead of a position, train-the-trainer roles and responsibilities can be seen as a function of an employee's responsibilities. The train-the-trainer's job is to specialize in preparing other staff for either one-on-one or group roles in learning activities and instruction and assistance. A train-the-trainer employee is helpful to all training job functions, even if the person is not responsible for teaching. For example, a resident expert might need assistance in getting someone to focus, explain, or identify primary issues. The train-the-trainer can educate all training employees about how to work with those coming to them for assistance. The train-the-trainer position holder typically has teaching or presentation experience, specifically in adult learning, and although much of the work can be done virtually or digitally, specialists must be able to determine the best mode or method for connecting with an employee—and although they might do so virtually or digitally, it is also often done face-to-face or in person.

Education Counselors

Counselors are staff identified as senior in the learning functions of the organization. They have extensive experience or education in teaching and learning and are considered resource people who can be one-on-one advisors to managers and employees attempting to design employee-training plans. They may advise councils, committees, or specialists who are trying to match activities to needs or to identify trends. Thus, they might be called in to advise councils or committees as well as individual employees. They are not involved in the evaluation process of the employees they counsel. Much of the work and discussion can be done virtually or digitally.

Mentors

Mentor programs in organizations identify employees who can be ongoing resource people teamed one-on-one with new or retrained employees. They meet with, answer questions for, and maintain ongoing dialogue with their mentees. Mentors are sounding boards for questions or issues. They advise employees assigned to them on overall job responsibilities. Mentor relationships have defined timelines; they typically last through a project, for a year, or through a performance period. Mentors are not involved in the evaluation process of the employees they mentor. Much of the work and discussion can be done virtually or digitally.

Coaches

Typically project-oriented, coaches are identified for their content knowledge and their skill in working with staff to get the job or process done. Coaches may have gone through a project before and are assigned to a work group or employee throughout a project. Although assigned to individuals, coaches typically do not join in the evaluation process of those they coach, but they may report back or comment on project timelines and success. Much of the work and discussion can be done virtually or digitally.

Peer Training

Coaching between or among employees of similar competencies, education, or experience, rather than by experts or a coach, is particularly effective for learning skills or abilities related to the workplace. These peer-training relationships can also be used for reflection or study following training (much like study groups in educational settings) and for observations following activities in which staff have to practice, such as in providing customer service or in handling problem patrons.

Although much of the work can be done virtually or digitally, specialists must be able to determine what is the best mode or method for connecting with an employee, and although they might do so virtually or digitally, it is also often done face-to-face or in person.

Content Experts

If organizations do choose one or some of the internal positions described thus far, or if they do not choose to identify and define multi-employee levels, at the very least they should identify content experts and design experts (both internal and external to the organization). For example, a small library might have a content expert to turn to when reviewing technical instructions to use in training staff or when reviewing an employee's learning plan. This person might look at workshop content or review the agenda of a conference to determine which programs might benefit the organization and which a staff member might report back on. Content experts might provide input to identify performance gaps, clarify training needs, and assist in mapping out a training approach; review, revise, or organize content; supply the content or offer ideas for those designing content; and review content for accuracy and completeness.

Content Designers

Content designers might be members of the training employees or councils or committees, or they might be outside designers who offer a commercial service. Their responsibilities could include facilitating the needs assessment process by defining target training needs and mapping out a training approach; working with content specialists to find appropriate training content; taking the training content and organizing, designing, or scripting it; reviewing the training content for consistency and clarity; and ensuring that there is a match between the audience and the delivery and techniques of the training content.

JOB TITLES, JOB DESCRIPTIONS, AND OTHER FACTORS RELATED TO INTERNAL TRAINING RESPONSIBILITIES

Although a list of who and how is relatively simple to bring to a planning discussion on learning, an organization must then change its job descriptions and position advertising, delineate benefits, and develop visions and statements and terminology for job performance for a training position. In addition, managers must adjust employee performance plans, employee goals and objectives, and organizational and departmental goals and objectives to reflect the new approach that places an emphasis on learning.

Finding and using the appropriate terminology is always tricky. Although organizations should review related terms in any umbrella organizations, a review of the literature from both the for-profit and the nonprofit worlds yields the following terminology to consider. The terminology chosen should be inserted into all job-related information, including job titles, position descriptions, ads, benefits statements, and if possible performance evaluations.

ADDITIONAL RESOURCES

IPL Especially for Librarians: Internet for Libraries—An excellent site, IPL's professional section with links to websites for staff development and training for librarians and library staff, much of the links chosen are specifically for libraryland (www.ipl.org).

Free Management Library—An in-depth site for all levels of managers in all types of libraries (http://managementhelp.org).

Library Support Staff—Although this site professes to be for support staff only, the content is very broad and recommended for a variety of types of libraries and all levels of employees (www.librarysupportstaff.com).

WebJunction—A combination of fee-based and free curriculum to assist employees throughout the organization. Although geared to public libraries in intent, this content is appropriate for all types of libraries (www.webjunction.org).

Appendix

Planning a Training and Development Infrastructure

Possible Job and Position Titles
- Training, education, and development specialist
- Continuous learning officer
- Continuing education specialist
- Manager of staff training or education and development
- Learning specialist

- Staff development specialist
- Professional development librarian
- Learning librarian
- Staff training, education, and development manager
- Technology training manager

Descriptions of Roles and Responsibilities

Although all job descriptions should include the responsibility of each employee to be committed to and active in learning activities, more specific descriptions of those with primary roles and responsibilities should be included in organizational content. Statements can also be enhanced by including a prioritized (e.g., 1, 2, 3) or ranking (e.g., primary, secondary) system, such as the percentage of time to be spent on the responsibility (e.g., 30 percent of an employee's responsibilities) or a profile of a typical week or month (e.g., one day a week is spent on X), as well as a list of specific activities for which staff may be totally or partially responsible. The following statements can be adapted for specific positions:

- Administers the employee development program, including planning, coordinating, and evaluating the systems and services to provide employees with support and resources in all areas of training, education, and development.
- Manages the teaching and learning environment.
- Spends 30 percent of time coordinating districtwide teaching and learning activities.
- Is responsible for staff training and development activities.
- Is responsible for the supervision and development of individual development plans.
- Coordinates mentoring or coaching programs.
- Develops train-the-trainer activities.
- Is responsible for the management of continuous-improvement activities, such as staff training or an electronic learning program for professional development or resident expert or mentor and coach programs.
- Is responsible for assessing, creating, and implementing technology training.

- Provides creative leadership in planning, developing, and administering information technology training programs.
- Trains employees across the organization.
- Acts in the capacity of the staff development officer.
- Is responsible for administering the training and development program, including skills assessment, curriculum identification, and the design of teaching and learning activities.
- Responsible for research and teaching.
- Serves as primary systems training and resource person.
- Plans, delivers, facilitates, and assesses research services and instruction provided to students, faculty, and staff.
- Plans, delivers, facilitates, and assesses technology support services provided to students, faculty, and staff.
- Provides leadership in designing, maintaining, and learning library goals and strategies that support the mission, visions, and goals of the library.
- Investigates and implements new technologies for staff learning, education, and development.
- Fulfills a campus leadership position to develop, coordinate, and support creative use of educational technologies within the library for staff learning.
- Selects, installs, and trains in the use of multimedia resources.
- Provides leadership in the planning, development, and provision of innovative, proactive learning, training, education, and development activities in a rapidly changing information environment.
- Provides development support for digital projects to all staff.
- Demonstrates knowledge of the application of new technologies to the delivery of training, education, and development activities for staff throughout the organization.

Required/Preferred Language for Position Statements

Depending on the position description, the following might be listed in the required or referred categories of the job ad:

- Excellent communication skills suitable for dealing with an environment that combines consulting, training, and research
- Knowledge and experience in organizational and staff development

- Knowledge of continuous-improvement techniques
- Experience in giving workshops or presentations
- Experience in training and development
- Knowledge of and experience in training, education, and development activities for professional and paraprofessional staff
- Experience in electronic learning environments
- Knowledge of principles and techniques of training and development
- Vision and leadership to facilitate library faculty teams in curriculum development and the integration of current and emerging technologies as they contribute to users' instructional needs
- Further graduate study in educational technology or a related field
- Knowledge of distance learning or computer-based technology
- Proficiency in teaching and the ability to structure learning experiences
- Planning, implementing, and assessing projects or programs, such as electronic information retrieval systems and microcomputer applications, especially in a reference and research environment
- A successful record of leadership, collaboration, and effective communication of technology to a range of audiences; knowledge of and experience in collaborative learning experience with group teaching
- Appropriate experience in the application of emerging technologies to staff training, education, and development
- The ability to troubleshoot hardware and software problems
- Strong analytical, communication, and interpersonal skills
- The ability to troubleshoot in Windows and Unix environments
- An advanced degree in librarianship, business, instructional technology, or a personnel-related field
- Superior oral and written communication skills
- The ability to train and develop library staff
- Knowledge of emerging training and development technologies and education theory
- Knowledge of and experience with distance learning
- Knowledge of and experience in instructional methods, adult learning, and education
- Enthusiastic participation in the library's continuous-learning environment
- Knowledge of and enthusiasm for a continuous-learning environment

Benefits Statements

Although all organizations should strive for benefits with a commitment to continuous learning, job ads should include appropriate benefits statements such as the following:

- Budget available for training and professional development (competitive process)
- Training and development support
- Support for research, training, and development
- Tuition reimbursement
- Continuing education opportunities, including tuition, conference, and institute support
- Knowledge or skill-based pay

External Opportunities

Although internal opportunities for training are numerous, managers also need to assess the environment for external learning opportunities. External opportunities are necessary for a wide variety of reasons:

- Many libraries are too small and have too few employees to have either full-time or part-time internal employee committed to training.
- Many libraries are too small and have only volunteers who are not appropriate for teaching and learning responsibilities.
- Some umbrella library organizations (e.g., cities, counties, colleges, universities, businesses) are committed to outsourcing nonprimary or support functions, such as teaching and learning activities.
- Managers may not have the employee talent necessary for training internal trainers.
- Organizational structures may prohibit changing job descriptions to include roles and responsibilities for teaching and learning, such as unions.
- Training topics may be identified that are most appropriately taught by those outside the organization.
- Organizations may not have the time to train internal employees in new, general, or specific competencies.

Although most managers are already knowledgeable about outside or non-organizational training, there are an increasing number of creative opportunities. These include the following print, in-person, and online or virtual and digital resources:

State libraries

Other state agencies—Many state agencies will allow other agency constituents to attend development and training offerings and annual programs. These tend to be as cost effective as state library fees. Some states have separate state agencies for libraries while others have departments, units, or divisions of other agencies. These opportunities could come from a single department or from anywhere in the larger umbrella agency. For example, a library department with a state agency for education could piggyback on opportunities in the broader service area.

Library schools—Once providing only in-person or in-town opportunities, many library schools now take their services on the road either through in-person offerings or through distance learning (classroom and individualized or self-directed instruction).

Educational institutions—Many teacher-only training opportunities have been opened up to non-K-12 educators in regional or geographically distributed service centers both for in-person and teleconference training.

Commercial ventures—Commercial or for-profit training opportunities offer content applicable to the nonprofit world, especially on the information environment (e.g., technology, customer service). Many commercial providers are also specializing in information environment content (technology and management).

Consortiums—Many libraries belong to state or regional consortiums to provide support functions and to oversee state and federal funding. Most of these arrangements offer training to members as well. Their training supports the basic functions they offer, and many have extensive annual or member- or needs-driven training. Although these arrangements may be specific to only one type of library, some are multi-type, and many more are opening their operations up to area or regional libraries for basic services and especially for training.

Partnerships—Although the concept of partnerships may be inherent in all the environments or opportunities listed previously, partnerships are now being formed exclusively to offer training for their library partners. Some of these partnerships are formal arrangements, and others are informal, based on the idea "this looks good, let's share costs and bring this person or institute in."

What Do Managers Need to Know about Staff?

Not only do managers need to gather information about staff training needs; they must also gather information about staff members themselves. This information assists managers in choosing training activities, selecting outside trainers, or identifying which internal staff will participate in which levels or areas of training. Necessary information includes the following:

- Employee learning styles and preferences regarding what training is offered and whether it is mandatory primary or secondary job responsibilities
- Employee preferences for learning settings, such as self-directed or individualized or group abilities to learn well together
- Teaching styles
- Experience in developing training materials and curriculum
- Competency levels, such as elementary knowledge of X or intermediate skills and abilities in Y
- Interest levels
- Rhythms for learning, such as best time of day for teaching or learning
- Expectations for learning
- Management expectations for employee performance

How Do Managers Select Internal Trainers and External Training Opportunities?

Selecting internal staff to be trainers or to be involved in any one of the myriad external training opportunities involves matching needs to talents or offerings. Whether the organization chooses internal or external trainers, in general, organizations are looking for individuals with presentation skills; individuals who are familiar with training, teaching, and education in general; employees who have concern for other employees; those who are familiar with and can distinguish between organizational theory to practice; those who have the confidence to design and deliver content; and those who have a commitment to learning in organizations. The processes for selecting such individuals follow.

Steps in Selecting Internal Trainers

1. Assess the organization's training needs.
2. Decide on internal levels and commitments.
3. Redo job descriptions.
4. Create job ads and interview schedules.
5. Interview internal employees.
6. Assess internal employees for training competencies.
7. Assess internal employees for related organizational development competencies, such as organization, communication, and time management to possibly manage the process of training.
8. Design a training plan for the train-the-trainers.

Steps in Selecting External Trainers

1. Prepare goals and objectives for training needs.
2. Prepare a statement explaining employees' training needs and management expectations (e.g., request for proposal, scenarios, employees profiles).
3. Prepare ads.
4. Design an interview schedule.
5. Design criteria for scoring and matching needs to trainers' curricula vitae and competencies. Evaluate media proposed, training setting, teaching styles, and original or designed curriculum.
6. Assess needed preparation, including any pre- or post-testing.
7. Participate in designing evaluations for training opportunities.
8. Assess needed follow-up or practice.
9. Match charges and costs to the budget available.

Providing additional or specific training for employees who wish to take on teaching and learning roles includes the following:

- Membership in teaching and learning and training organizations (e.g., the American Society for Training and Development and its local and regional chapters) to participate in in-person and online regional and national conferences, and seminars as well as online publications
- Teaching and learning and train-the-trainer continuing education in higher education, including courses in adult education

- Self-directed study with written and media and audiovisual content
- Self-assessment with teaching and presentation experts, including consultants brought in to assess presentation skills and to develop a improvement plan
- Participation in association teaching and learning conference content, seminar, and immersion institutes

Whether managers and staff choose internal or external training, the Web is becoming an increasingly valuable resource for information about and the delivery of a wide variety of training opportunities. The sites listed in the "Additional Resources" section of this chapter offer resources for all sizes of libraries and all levels of commitment and budget.

Myntha Cuffy and Dorothy Marie Persson

chapter 14

Instructional Design in Library Settings

Designing Effective and Efficient Training Programs

STAFF DEVELOPMENT TAKES PLACE IN A VARIETY OF SETTINGS, both formal and informal, and many professionals, including some who might not fit the description of instructor or human resources personnel, find themselves creating instructional programs for staff. Training programs take many forms and can include activities such as sharing information from a conference with colleagues, teaching staff how to use the Intranet, demonstrating features of the Integrated Library System, or creating a program to promote multicultural understanding. A thoughtfully designed learner-centered approach to instruction can decrease anxiety and increase effectiveness, both for the instructor and the learner. Research on retention has demonstrated that ineffective instruction in staff development can breed dissatisfaction and lead to high turnover (Get the Right People, 2007). A design approach to staff development goes beyond content to consider the totality of the instructional endeavor, from the people involved to the problem to be solved and possible solutions and program evaluation. This chapter provides an introduction to and overview of the popular Analysis, Design, Development, Implementation, and Evaluation (ADDIE) model of instructional design for librarians and human resources professionals who are new to instructional design.

The ADDIE model describes instructional design in five steps: analysis, design, development, implementation, and evaluation (Allen, 2006). The model has been the dominant force in instructional design since the post–World War II era, when it was developed as a process for increasing efficiency in the training of military personnel (Allen, 2006). At the same time, Benjamin Bloom (1956) was developing his *Taxonomy of Educational Objectives*, in which he identified and described different domains of learning (cognitive, affective, and psychomotor) and the ways these domains influence instructional objectives. The popularity of the ADDIE model can be attributed to its robust adaptability to instructional activities in each of these domains, as well as its applicability to a variety of organizations and training needs. For example, the Ohio State University Libraries adapted ADDIE to improve workflow in technical services (McGurr, 2008).

Critiques of ADDIE focus on its seemingly linear and rigid nature (Ruark, 2008) and the fact that strict adherence to the structure of the model may stifle innovation and preclude detection of necessary intermediate steps in the design process (Hokanson, Miller, & Hooper, 2008). Nevertheless, these critics recognize the value of a structured model and advocate for a reimagining and expansion of ADDIE that provides room for originality and critical reflection (Hokanson, Miller, & Hooper, 2008; Ruark, 2008). This chapter takes ADDIE as a framework, building on its simplicity and taking advantage of its adaptability to guide the designer through the design process without curtailing creativity. The instructional designer is encouraged throughout to contemplate the recursive nature of instructional design, to build additional steps into the model where useful, and to engage with the process in a thoughtful and reflective way. This chapter also takes into account recent research on the importance of integrating motivational elements into design, an approach that emphasizes the primacy of the learner rather than the content to be learned and the reflexive nature of the design endeavor.

Step 1: Analysis

Analysis is the foundation of good design (Morrison, Ross, & Kemp, 2007). Analysis produces an understanding of the problem, an understanding without which any training activity is likely to be ineffective. The questions asked during the analysis phase of instructional design clarify the purpose for which and the situation in which instruction will take place. Smith and Ragan (2005) describe four elements for analysis, three of which should be clearly defined during the first stage of instructional design: the learner, the learning context, and the purpose of the learning task (the fourth element, evaluation, takes place at the end of the instructional process):

1. Consider the learners. Each question should be answered as completely as possible, through interaction with the unit requesting the training. Documentation can take the form of spreadsheets, notes, and so on.
   - Who are the learners? Are they managers? Line staff? A mix? What is their role in the organization?
   - What do they already know?
   - What can they already do?
   - What do they need to know?
   - What do they need to be able to do?
   - Where will they be located when they are learning? Are they traveling to a remote site that is unfamiliar to them?
   - Will their participation be voluntary? Recommended? Mandatory?
   - Will they be participating in other learning activities immediately before or after this instructional module? (For example, is this instruction part of an orientation program, and if so, at what stage of orientation will it take place?)

2. Next, consider the context in which instruction is likely to take place.
   - Will instruction take place on site, or will learners be traveling to a new place?
   - How much time will the instructor and the learners have?
   - Will there be access to technology, and to what degree is this important?
   - Will they have individual learning stations?
   - What is the culture of the organization or subunit providing the instruction? Although decisions about the delivery method will be made later on, questions about this aspect of the project may also be asked during the initial analysis.

3. Finally, consider the purpose of the instruction.
   - What is the problem the instruction is designed to solve?
   - What is the nature of the problem?

Bloom (1956) suggested that the nature of an instructional problem could be conceptualized according to one of three domains. Problems in the cognitive domain relate to knowledge and information. Problems in the affective domain relate to attitudes and values. Problems in the psychomotor domain relate to tasks and skills. The mode of instruction varies for each of these domains (see table 14.1). Another way to conceptualize the nature of the problem is to describe the nature of the knowledge the learner should have at the end of instruction. Declarative knowledge is information that can be stated or described. Demonstrative knowledge is the ability to perform a task.

Table 14.1

INSTRUCTIONAL DOMAINS

DOMAIN	OBJECTIVE	EXAMPLE	DELIVERY FORMAT
Psychomotor	Perform a task	The learner will complete a circulation transaction.	Simulation, demonstration
Cognitive	Gain knowledge, become informed	The learner will understand the management structure of technical services.	Question and answer, concept mapping, recall
Affective	Develop an attitude	The learner will gain appreciation for diversity.	Group discussions, role play, storytelling

To fully understand the purpose of the instruction, the instructional designer should also develop an understanding of the ways in which the problem has been addressed in the past. How have other methods of addressing the problem been successful or unsuccessful?

Say, for example, that the purpose of the training program is to teach staff how to use the Integrated Library System. It is important to understand what has already been done to meet that need. What has worked? Where are the opportunities for change or improvement?

Learning objectives should be clearly defined and, where possible, clearly related to observable outcomes. Objectives should be focused on what the learner will experience and do rather than on what the instructor will present or do (e.g., the learner will learn the primary circulation functions rather than the instructor demonstrating the primary circulation functions). This subtle difference may seem unimportant, but it creates a context for valid evaluation. Instead of asking whether the instructor did some particular thing, the evaluation question at the end of the instructional event will relate to what the learner knows or does not know.

Asking these questions during the initial analysis will also be beneficial during the design phase, as they prepare the instructional designer to clearly describe relationships between what the learner already knows and can do and what the learner will be learning.

The question of purpose relates to both design and evaluation. If the purpose of instruction is for the learner to develop customer service skills or practice empathy or embrace a spirit of inclusiveness, how will these directives be defined and demonstrated? It is essential for the organization, the designer, and the learner to know not only what the learner knows but also *that* the learner knows. This relates back to the issue of retention: learners feel more satisfied and value their learning more highly when they can express exactly what it is they have learned and how it applies to the work they perform (Get the Right People, 2007). All who are invested in the outcome of instruction need to know that the learner actually learned. Objectives created in the early analysis phase will be essential in later determining whether the desired learning took place. "The output of the front-end-analysis stage of design is a clear description of the learning environment, the learners, and the learning task" (Smith & Ragan, 1993, p. 95).

Step 2: Design

Design takes into account the total learning situation, encompassing the aesthetic but going beyond issues of look and feel to consider the context in which learning will take place (Smith & Ragan, 1993). The questions asked in the design phase will pave the way for instruction that is effective, efficient, and appealing:

- What are the options for teaching the material?
- What is the best fit considering the environmental factors revealed and the objectives developed in the analysis phase?

- What are the benefits and consequences of different models, such as online modules, in-class instruction, and group versus individual instruction?

The answers to these questions will relate directly to the type of knowledge and skills the instructor is planning to impart, the location of learners (remote versus on-site), and the availability of instructors. Simple, sequential tasks can be taught effectively using online modules. Complex cognitive tasks and skills in the affective domain may be taught effectively in small-group settings that provide opportunities for role play and conversation (Morrison, Ross, & Kemp, 2007).

Engaging the senses can increase the effectiveness of instruction. Finding ways to incorporate sound, visuals, group interaction, and humor can aid in both attentiveness and retention. Bloom (1956) identifies five levels of attention, beginning with the learner simply receiving information and progressing through responding to it, valuing the information, committing to it, organizing it, and finally embracing it as part of a larger value system. Aesthetic elements can aid the learner in attending to material as it is being presented, which paves the way for the rest of the process.

Step 3: Development

During the development phase, the instructional designer will work to create a logic or rhythm for the program. A thoughtful consideration of the situations in which the training will be used can help the instructional designer find ways to simulate those situations in training. Questions to ask during the development phase include the following:

- What is the most logical sequence for presenting this information?
- What assumptions are being made about what the learner already knows?
- Where might there be gaps in the learner's knowledge, and how can those gaps be filled in?
- To what degree does this module relate to the objectives identified in the analysis phase?
- Is the module appropriate to the identified audience?

Asking these questions allows the instructional designer to build a natural bridge from the known to the unknown, from skills in hand to skills that will be developed, and to exploit every opportunity to demonstrate the relationships between what the learner already knows and what the learner will be learning. A review of the issues revealed during the analysis phase is an important part of the development phase.

The development phase can be regarded as a detailed expansion of identified objectives. Objectives are often expressed in terms of what the learner will know or be able to do at the end of the educational encounter. During the development phase these objectives are expanded in detail to describe the steps the learner will take to meet the objective. This process not only clarifies the objective but also reveals potential gaps in instruction and sets the stage for evaluation. One way of beginning to expand objectives is to take the declaration of what the learner will do and change it into a question of how the learner will do it. For example, "The learner will know how to use the staff side of the Online Public Access Catalog" can be described instead as "How will the learner know how to use the staff side of the Online Public Access Catalog?" The answer to that question includes a comprehensive level of detail to reveal potential gaps in the instruction.

Consider the following example of directions for the first step in an interlibrary loan training program hosted on a local intranet:

Weak	*Strong*
• Sign into the staff intranet and select the interlibrary-loan learning module.	• Open a web browser, such as Internet Explorer or Mozilla Firefox.
	• Go to http://libraryintranet.org.
	• Sign in using your organizational ID and password.
	• On the upper left side of the first page, click on "Groups." A drop-down menu will appear.
	• Select "Interlibrary Loan."
	• Select "Learning Module."

Although it will not always be necessary to articulate this level of detail to the learner, an exhaustive outline of necessary steps will reveal any gaps in instruction, as well as unconsciously made assumptions about what the learner already knows.

Definitions of success should be included in each of the objectives. Simply stating that the learner will know how to complete an interlibrary-loan transaction is not as clear an objective as stating that, upon receipt of an interlibrary-loan request, the learner will (1) prepare a complete bibliographic citation for the requested item, (2) use appropriate resources to determine ownership of the requested item, and (3) send the interlibrary-loan request to the provider library using the appropriate form. Only when success is clearly defined can it be accurately measured.

Step 4: Implementation

Implementation should be coupled with close observation and documentation. The instructor should be aware of and able to report on what is and is not working, aspects of the program that seem awkward or unclear, and questions learners are asking that were not anticipated in the model.

Step 5: Evaluation

How will success be defined and measured? The success or failure of the instructional endeavor is based on whether—and to what degree—objectives were achieved. In social science literature, validity is the degree to which evaluation methods actually measure the domain they purport to measure. For example, a task designed to measure staff cohesiveness should measure staff cohesiveness, not cooperation on a task. Validity in instructional design is an issue at every step: Is the problem that has been identified the real problem? Are the methods that are being used appropriate for the identified need? Are the evaluation methods actually evaluating the effectiveness of the instruction?

As mentioned earlier, the ADDIE model provides opportunities for evaluation at the completion of each stage (Smith & Ragan, 2005). Formative evaluation takes place throughout the design process, and serves "to confirm the accuracy of the design process at each stage" (Smith & Ragan, 2005, p. 328). Summative evaluation takes place at the completion of instruction and involves the collection and analysis of data for the purpose of drawing conclusions about the success of the instructional endeavor. Just as the mode of instruction varies for each learning domain (psychomotor, cognitive, and affective), so will the mode of evaluation differ (see table 14.2). The question that guides summative evaluation is: did the instruction meet the identified need? In other words, did the learner learn? The evaluation techniques chosen to find the answer to this question depend on the mode of instruction.

Table 14.2

INSTRUCTIONAL DOMAINS AND METHODS FOR SUMMATIVE EVALUATION

DOMAIN	OBJECTIVE	EXAMPLE	DELIVERY FORMAT	EVALUATION
Psychomotor	Perform a task	The learner will complete a circulation transaction.	Simulation, demonstration	Skill test, observation
Cognitive	Gain knowledge, become informed	The learner will understand the management structure of technical services.	Question and answer, concept mapping, recall	Knowledge test
Affective	Develop an attitude	The learner will gain appreciation for diversity.	Group discussions, role play, storytelling	Observation, interviews

Practical considerations will also influence the decision regarding mode of evaluation. Will the learner have time to participate in an evaluative interview? Is the instructor available to observe the learner putting skills to use after the instruction has taken place?

Conclusion

A systematic approach to instructional design can decrease anxiety for the instructor and can increase retention and satisfaction in the learner. As advances in technology lead to new developments in instruction and training, a flexible model such as the one presented here can serve the needs of a variety of organizations and learning situations, and it can prepare the instructional designer to take advantage of opportunities for increasing the efficiency and effectiveness of training for a changing world. The flexibility of the ADDIE model means that it can evolve as technology evolves and as new teaching and learning paradigms are discovered.

REFERENCES

Allen, W. C. (2006). "Overview and Evolution of the ADDIE Training System." *Advances in Developing Human Resources, 8,* 430–442. Retrieved from http://adh.sage pub.com

Bloom, B. S. (1956). *Taxonomy of Educational Objectives: The Classification of Educational Goals, by a Committee of College and University Examiners.* New York, NY: D. McKay.

"Get the Right People and Keep Them Engaged." (2007, January). *Human Resources, 9.* doi:1196500671

Hokanson, B., Miller, C., & Hooper, S. R. (2008). "Role-Based Design: A Contemporary Perspective for Innovation in Instructional Design." *TechTrends: Linking Research and Practice to Improve Learning, 52,* 36–43. doi:10.1007/s11528-008-0215-0

McGurr, M. (2008). "Improving the Flow of Materials in a Cataloging Department: Using ADDIE for a Project in the Ohio State University Libraries." *Library Resources and Technical Services, 52*(2), 54–60. Retrieved from www.ftrf.org/ala/mgrps/divs/alcts/resources/lrts/index.cfm

Morrison, G. R., Ross, S. M., & Kemp, J. E. (2007). *Designing Effective Instruction* (5th ed.). Hoboken, NJ: Wiley.

Ruark, B. E. (2008). "ISD Model Building: From Tabula Rasa to Apple Peel." *Performance Improvement, 47*(7), 24–30. doi:1717779071

Smith, P. L., & Ragan, T. J. (1993). *Instructional Design.* New York, NY: Merrill.

Smith, P. L., & Ragan, T. J. (2005). *Instructional Design* (3rd ed.). Hoboken, NJ: Wiley.

ADDITIONAL RESOURCES

Armstrong, A. (2004). *Instructional Design in the Real World: A View from the Trenches.* Hershey, PA: Information Science.

Cowell, C., Hopkins, P. C., McWhorter, R., & Jorden, D. L. (2006). "Alternative Training Models." *Advances in Developing Human Resources, 8,* 460–475. doi:10.1177/1523422306292945

Hodell, C. (Ed.). (2006). *ISD from the Ground Up: A No-Nonsense Approach to Instructional Design* (2nd ed.). Alexandria, VA: ASTD Press.

Houghton-Jan, S. (2007). "Assessing Staff on the Competencies." *Library Technology Reports, 43,* 44–47. Retrieved from www.alatechsource.org/ltr

Lubans, J., Jr. (2009). "What? So What? Now What?" *Library Leadership and Management, 23*(3), 140–149. Retrieved from www.ala.org/ala/mgrps/divs/llama/publications/llandm/libraryleadership.cfm

Munro, R. A., & Rice-Munro, E. (2004). "Learning Styles, Teaching Approaches, and Technology." *Journal for Quality and Participation, 27*, 26–32. Retrieved from www.asq.org/pub/jqp

Reed, L., & Signorelli, P. (2008). "Are You Following Me?" *American Libraries, 39*, 42–45. Retrieved from www.ala.org/ala/alonline/index.cfm

Ware, J., Craft, R., & Kerschenbaum, S. (2007). "Training Tomorrow's Workforce." *Training and Development, 61*, 58–60. Retrieved from www.astd.org/TD

Chad F. Boeninger

chapter 15 / # Using Online Videos for Staff Training

OR MANY PEOPLE, ONE OF THE MOST EFFECTIVE METHODS TO learn a new skill is to have someone teach them that skill in person. However, in-person training is not always a practical solution, as there may be certain challenges in bringing staff members together with a trainer. To remedy this, many trainers create guides with screenshots and annotations to facilitate staff members in learning a new skill on their own time and at their own pace. A quick look at library websites across the Internet will reveal web pages, screenshots, and tutorials that demonstrate how to use the databases and online catalogs that libraries provide to their users. Although these guides can be very effective in teaching staff new skills, they can be very time consuming to create and perhaps difficult to use. Web video is an excellent alternative to creating traditional training documents. With web video, trainers can create content quickly and efficiently that meets the needs of users in a timely manner. Users can then watch a skill being demonstrated on the computer screen and can replay the video as necessary to better understand the skill. This chapter discusses how library trainers can use web video to create training and help content for their end users.

One of the more traditional methods of training end users is to create guides with screenshots of a database demonstration with annotations. These guides are often HTML web pages, PDF files, or Microsoft Word documents. Guides in this format can be downloaded, e-mailed, or printed so that users can access and use them in a variety of ways. When creating these types of guides, the creator usually takes screenshots of the database, edits them in an image-editing application (e.g., Photoshop, GNU Image Manipulation Program [GIMP]) and then places the image in a Word document or HTML file. The creator then must annotate the images to demonstrate what the pictures are supposed to teach the user. For a guide to be useful for end users, the creator must think carefully about what screenshots and text he or she will need in order to effectively communicate what is to be learned. Also, because the screenshots are not a live demonstration of the web application or database, the creator must choose to take screen captures of the most important information. Unfortunately, often the most important information is relative and can vary with each user. Although traditional guides can be an effective method of training end users, they do have several limitations for both the content creator and the end user.

Video, in contrast, can offer the trainer a faster, more efficient method to provide instruction. With video, trainers can use the same methods to demonstrate a resource that they would use if they were to teach someone how to do something in person. Video allows trainers to capture everything that they would normally demonstrate, without requiring them to be selective about what they capture. The trainer does not have to decide which screens to capture as images, because a video will record and display everything. Also, because video captures the trainer's voice as well as the actions on screen, the trainer does not have to worry about the best way to annotate screenshot images. The trainer simply has to show and explain in real time and record the screens for the user. In other words, the technology of video recording does not demand that the trainer decide what should be included and what should be left out; with video, the trainer can easily record and show anything that he or she wants the user to learn.

Although there are several applications that record computer screens, because of the scope of this guide, this chapter focuses on only one application. Screencast-O-Matic is one of the easiest tools to use to record a computer screen to show users how something is done. The name of the program is derived from the term *screencast*, which means to record a computer screen and share it with others through web video. Screencast-O-Matic enables a trainer to record a computer browser, a computer application, or anything on the computer desktop via an easy-to-use web browser interface. One simply has to point the Internet browser to www.screencast-o-matic.com and click the "Create" button to get started. On the "Create" screen, the user will have options to adjust the recording size and the audio input device, and can even choose whether to include a small video from a webcam in the screen recording. Please note that the application requires Java to run. If Java is not installed on the computer, a link to download the Java application is displayed on the screen. Because Screencast-O-Matic requires only a web browser and Java to run, it can run on both Mac and Windows computers.

Unlike more complex recording tools such as Adobe Captivate and TechSmith's Camtasia, the free version of Screencast-O-Matic does not have options for annotating your video with text, arrows, or other visual cues. Therefore, it is absolutely important when recording a video with Screencast-O-Matic that the trainer use some sort of audio-input device. To record audio, the trainer can use a dedicated microphone or the microphone included with a webcam. One should note that better audio quality comes at a price; you can get decent and usable audio from a webcam, but you will likely be more satisfied with sound captured from a dedicated microphone. For example, USB microphones, such as the Blue Snowball (www.bluemic.com/snowball) work very well for screen recordings.

Screencast-O-Matic is available in a free and in a pro version. The free version limits recording time to fifteen minutes (more than enough for almost all purposes) and includes a watermark advertising Screencast-O-Matic.com in the bottom left of all exported videos. As of this writing, the pro version of Screencast-O-Matic is priced at nine dollars a year, and in addition to removing the watermark, it provides the options of password-protected videos, editing tools, and sixty-minute recording times.

Once the trainer has recorded the training video, he or she must next find a place to put it so that others may watch it. For most, YouTube is the first choice that comes to mind. YouTube is the largest and most popular host of video content in the world. YouTube continues to make it easier for contributors to upload their videos, and the site allows nearly all types of user-generated content. Before the days of YouTube and other video-hosting sites, content creators had to do their own file conversions for their video and then place the video file on their sites for users to download. YouTube allows users to upload almost any video file type, and the site does the conversion and hosting for users for free. Once YouTube has converted the file, the trainer can send users a link to the video or embed the entire video on the training website.

One YouTube feature that trainers may want to use is the ability to create custom playlists of videos. A trainer can go to his or her YouTube video page and organize the videos there into playlists. As an example, if a trainer wanted to show users collections for videos about researching company information resources, he or she could put all of the videos on that topic in a playlist of company information resources. Likewise, the trainer could create an industry information resources playlist with different videos. The videos in the playlists can be reordered in whatever way the trainer wants the users to view them, thus allowing for customized, sequential viewing of training content. Trainers can then share the playlists by sending users a link or embedding the playlists on a web page. Trainers may also add videos created by other YouTube users to their own playlists, thus allowing them to create custom training modules. Figure 15.1 is an example of a playlist that can be embedded or shared.

Figure 15.1: Sample Video Playlist

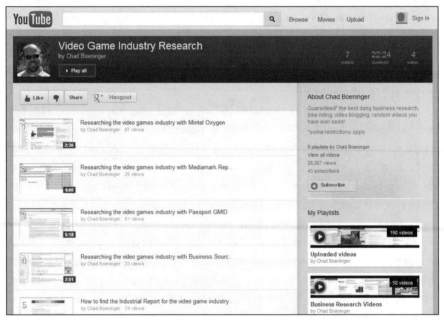

YouTube is often referred to as the Internet's second-largest search engine, after Google. As such, it is likely that other YouTube users will find a trainer's videos, even if they are not the intended audience. In most circumstances this is not a big deal and could even be considered a form of library outreach. After all, what better way to inform the average Internet user of the things libraries do than through a YouTube video? However, there may be times when a trainer wants to make a video private so that only the intended audience can watch it. YouTube allows content producers to make their videos private or unlisted to limit who watches them. According to YouTube, setting a video to "private" will allow content producers to choose up to fifty users who are allowed to watch the video. Unfortunately, this method requires that each member of the trainer's intended audience has a YouTube account and that the trainer knows each member's YouTube account user name. Perhaps a simpler way to make videos inaccessible to the general public is to designate them "unlisted." With this method, a trainer could send the audience the link to the video via e-mail even if they do not have YouTube accounts, and only those with the URL would be able to watch the video. The trainer could also post the URL on a private intranet as well. Unlisted videos are excluded from the public YouTube videos and therefore will not show up on search results page.

Tools like Screencast-o-Matic and YouTube make it so easy that anyone can create a video and post it to the Internet. Although video enables a trainer to easily record anything that he or she wants to, the trainer will produce better learning videos with careful planning. The first suggestion in planning a video is to create a basic outline with what you would like to demonstrate in a video. Because most training videos are not Hollywood productions, try to keep the process as simple as possible. You don't have to create a complicated storyboard with scenes, scripts, and more. Because many ideas for training videos often come from questions that the trainer receives frequently, he or she probably already has a pretty good idea what should be addressed in the video. Regardless of how well the trainer knows the topic or the question being addressed, it is still a very good idea to create an outline. An outline will help in planning the content and the pacing of the video. If you do not want to edit your video clips and prefer recording on track of video during one take, then an outline is essential. Without the outline you may find yourself forgetting a key element, which would require you to go back and record the same video again. Practice makes perfect, but speaking from experience, recording the same track over and over can get old quickly. A simple outline on a sticky note may be all you need to keep your video recording on track.

It is also a good idea to keep outlines for content even if the video will not be produced until much later. Because a trainer may have to set aside some time to make a video, he or she cannot always make a video as soon as it is needed or as soon as the idea comes to mind. Likewise, a single concept may be too insignificant to make a video for it, but a collection of smaller concepts might be more worthwhile for both the trainer and the end user. Keeping a bank of video topic outlines is a great way to make sure ideas actually make it from concept to the computer screen. You can also use the outline bank to prioritize which videos should be made first and which ones need more thought or development.

An outline also allows the trainer to see when he or she is attempting to squeeze too much into a single video. When making a web video, it is important to keep the videos as short as possible. For example, I attempt to keep all of my instructional videos less than five minutes in length. The scope and content covered often determine the length of the video, but try to keep the video around five minutes or less so that users can quickly understand the concept you are trying to teach. This is often a challenge, as we have a tendency to give users as much information as possible in the training exercise. Video hosts like YouTube and others are allowing longer videos to be uploaded, so it may be tempting to max out the ten- to fifteen-minute time limit on your uploaded videos. (Some hosting services allow up to two hours.) However, it is strongly suggested that if you find yourself going over the five-minute mark, it might be a good idea to break your longer video down into shorter ones. The videos could then be grouped together in a customized playlist, allowing the user to play the videos in the order assigned by the trainer.

Shorter videos also allow users to watch the training in short bursts. Because you are using video to record training information, it is likely that your users do not have large blocks of time to watch long videos. Shorter videos, organized in playlists or modules on a website, allow users to more easily watch the video training at a pace that works for them. Finally, using shorter video segments makes it easier for the trainer to update, change, delete, or replace content. This is especially important in videos that demonstrate library database and application interfaces. It never fails that right after you have made a video series demonstrating a database, the vendor updates the interface. If you have used shorter videos, you might not have to replace every single video, just the ones affected by the changes.

One of the most important advantages of web video over text-based training guides is the concept of personality. Typical text-based documentation may do a great job of training people in how to do something, but those documents can never come close to the personal engagement of video. Web video gives the trainer, the expert, a literal voice. Many training videos do not take full advantage of the personal nature of video. Trainers should recognize that video really is an excellent opportunity to engage with their audience. When beginning a training video, a trainer should introduce him- or herself quickly, followed immediately by a quick summary of what users will learn in the next four to five minutes while watching the video. Although it is entirely optional, I often choose to do a personal video shot while introducing myself and the topic, and then transition into the on-screen demonstration. At the end of the demonstration, the video then transitions back to me, where I suggest ways to get in touch with me if users have questions. I shoot the personal video with an inexpensive handheld camera, such as a Flip video camcorder. The camera clips are joined with the Screencast-O-Matic clips and edited together in Windows Live Movie Maker (Mac users could do the same with iMovie). I believe that this allows users to see the person and the face behind the video, and it allows me to demonstrate my expertise and highlight my personality. Such personal touches can also convey the trainer's confidence and authority in teaching the subject in the video. With text-based training guides, it is often difficult to determine the trainer's personality, expertise, and voice. With video, there is no question.

Regardless of the format of training materials, trainers do appreciate feedback on what they do. With web video, the trainer may not receive much immediate feedback. However, the trainer can look at statistics for the videos to see how and where the videos are being used. Most of the most popular video hosts, including YouTube, blip.tv, Viddler, and Vimeo, offer some type of service that records statistics for all the videos on the site. The hosts do record statistics differently, and often the types of statistics a trainer sees depends on whether he or she has a free or premium account with the video hosting service. How-

Figure 15.2: Sample Locations of Video Usage

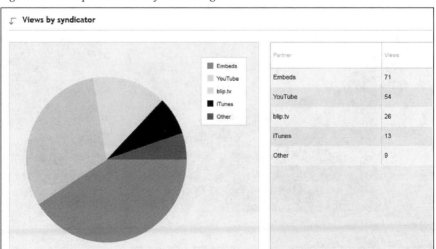

ever, regardless of the video host used, statistics can provide valuable insight into how the video is being watched.

As an example, blip.tv records how each video is viewed. This allows the trainer to see where the video is getting used the most and which places may need to be promoted more. Figure 15.2 demonstrates the locations of a video.

In Figure 15.2, the video is viewed most when it is embedded on the author's subject blog. The video has also been used in other places, as shown in the statistics for sites that have not been strongly promoted by the author. Blip.tv enables content creators to cross-post their videos to multiple destinations. One does not have to distribute videos to multiple locations, but I try to post the videos I produce in as many places as possible.

Blip.tv also records how much of the video is viewed. Blip.tv calls this statistic engagement, but other video-hosting services may have a different name for it. What the statistic shows is how much of your video users are watching. Figure 15.3 shows the engagement graph for blip.tv.

Figure 15.3 shows that approximately 45 percent of viewers watched 100 percent of the video. The figure shows a pretty flat graph, so there is not a noticeable place where viewers begin dropping off. A graph such as this, however, can show the time in a video at which the most users drop off. The engagement statistics can give trainers important information that they can use to

Figure 15.3 Engagement Graph for blip.tv

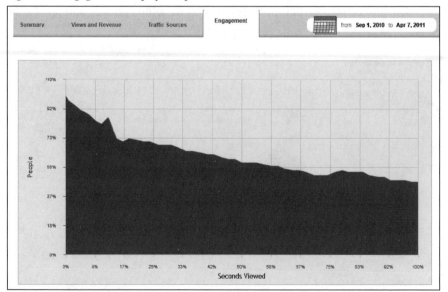

improve the quality of their videos. If there is a noticeable pattern of when viewers stop watching a video, the trainer can make adjustments to future recordings to change that behavior. The trainer may look to alter the pacing of the video, for example, to get the viewer into the video content more quickly.

Using web video for training does take a lot of practice, and one should not expect to be an expert right away. Although trainers should look at other videos for examples and guidance, they should not expect that their videos will turn out perfect on the first try. As a matter of fact, trainers should not attempt to aim for perfection when producing their videos. It is important to produce the best content possible, but trying to correct every single flaw in a video will slow down the video production process. In many cases, training content is time sensitive, so delaying the release of a video to perfect the content may not be beneficial to users in the long run.

With each video they make, trainers will get better and more efficient at making videos. Trainers should learn something from each experience that will make the next video easier to make. As they continue to produce videos, trainers will find different methods and tools that make the process even easier. When I first started, it took me more than two hours to make a single video. However, for a recent class, I was able to produce, edit, and upload four five-minute videos in just under an hour.

With practice, web video can be an extremely effective method of teaching users, as it allows them to learn at their own pace and on their own time. Web video also enables trainers to teach users with visual demonstrations, very similar to the way that they would deliver training content in person. Through the use of this technology, library trainers can add a more personal touch to training videos than they can with text-based training materials while potentially reaching more users than they could in a traditional classroom training session.

ADDITIONAL RESOURCES

Adolphus, M. (2009). "Using the Web to Teach Information Literacy." *Online, 33*(4), 20–25.

Brogan, C., & Smith, J. (2010). *Trust Agents: Using the Web to Build Influence, Improve Reputation, and Earn Trust* (Rev. ed.). Hoboken, NJ: Wiley.

Brown-Sica, M., Sobel, K., & Pan, D. (2009). "Learning for All: Teaching Students, Faculty, and Staff with Screencasting." *Public Services Quarterly, 5*(2), 81–97. doi:10.1080/15228950902805282

Charnigo, L. (2009). "Lights! Camera! Action! Producing Library Instruction Video Tutorials Using Camtasia Studio." *Journal of Library and Information Services in Distance Learning, 3*(1), 23–30. doi:10.1080/15332900902794880

Garfield, S. (2010). *Get Seen: Online Video Secrets to Building Your Business.* Hoboken, NJ: Wiley.

Handley, A., & Chapman, C. C. (2011). *Content Rules: How to Create Killer Blogs, Podcasts, Videos, Ebooks, Webinars (and More) that Engage Customers and Ignite your Business.* Hoboken, NJ: Wiley.

Kimok, D., & Heller-Ross, H. (2008). "Visual Tutorials for Point-of-Need Instruction in Online Courses." *Journal of Library Administration, 48*(3), 527–543.

Kroski, E. (2009). "That's Infotainment!" *School Library Journal, 55*(2), 40–42.

Oud, J. (2009). "Guidelines for Effective Online Instruction Using Multimedia Screencasts." *Reference Services Review, 37*(2), 164–177.

Slebodnik, M., & Riehle, C. F. (2009). "Creating Online Tutorials at Your Libraries: Software Choices and Practical Implications." *Reference and User Services Quarterly, 49*(1), 33–51.

Lila Daum Fredenburg

chapter 16

The Ideal

Joint Labor and Management Staff Development Programs

IN 2009 **WORKERS IN EDUCATION, TRAINING, AND LIBRARY OCCUPATIONS** had unionization rates of 38 percent, the highest rate for any occupation group. Unions represented roughly 29 percent of librarians and library technicians in 2009 (U.S. Bureau of Labor Statistics, 2010). Compared to 11.9 percent of workers represented by a union nationally (U.S. Bureau of Labor Statistics, 2010) it would seem that there should be an abundance of joint labor management training programs. This is especially true in the current economic environment, when employment growth is weak, technology is evolving faster than ever, and the need for worker training and retraining is so very apparent. Joint labor management training programs for librarians and library workers are not commonplace, despite widespread unionization of the profession. This chapter reviews examples of joint labor management training programs and why they are beneficial, as well as examples of joint programs in the library world.

Although examples of public-sector labor strife surfaced in several states in 2011, modern examples of workforce training and development through labor management cooperation have nevertheless emerged. Jointly operated training programs benefit not only the workers but also the employers and the communities they serve. Joint management training programs are different from government-sponsored programs targeted at unemployed or underemployed groups. They are also different from management-originated and sponsored training programs, which most often offer just-in-time training designed to teach very specific skills related to emerging technologies or workflows.

The long history and huge successes of jointly sponsored apprenticeship programs in the building trades should serve as a model for programs in libraries, despite the apparent disparity in the substantive skills required. Joint apprenticeship programs covering autoworkers, carpenters, electricians, plumbers, and cement masons date back to the 1940s, and their success is undisputed (U.S. Apprenticeship Development Links, n.d.). This long tradition of joint apprenticeship programs has even found a home in higher education, including at Indiana University (2006) and Yale University (2003), thus proving that the higher education environment need not be a deterrent.

Moreover, through their 2010 collective bargaining agreement, Yale University and the Federated University Employees committed themselves to long-term substantive labor management cooperative initiatives. These initiatives include joint training programs and best-practices initiatives developed on a cooperative basis (Yale University, 2009). In fact, the libraries at Yale have followed up on this concept and have formed a joint committee in the libraries to work on cooperative initiatives and best practices (D. Turner, then associate university librarian, Yale University Libraries, personal communication, September 9, 2010).

The most familiar area of jointly sponsored programs relate to health and safety. The passage of the Occupational Safety and Health Act in 1970 spawned the growth of labor management health and safety committees in all industries, including libraries. Many of these committees have done excellent work in sponsoring safety and ergonomic training initiatives. Yale University's (2010) labor management health and safety committee recently celebrated twenty years of cooperative efforts. Similar committees exist at Indiana University (2012), Michigan State University (2009), and Brown University (n.d.).

The UAW-Ford Education, Development, and Training Program (EDTP), distinct from its joint apprenticeship program, negotiated in 1982, were among the first and one of the most admired joint labor management training programs (UAW-Ford, n.d.). The EDTP was "hailed as a prototype of the kind of cooperatively–run institutions desperately needed in America" (Tomasko & Dickinson, 1991, p. 59). The Ford model began in the 1990s as a response to the need for worker retraining due to industry contraction and technological changes, and it soon spread to the construction, steel, transportation, health-care, and hotel industries (Van Buren, 2002). Many of these programs offered generalized training and could serve as models for libraries. In particular, the Pathways worker training and education programs negotiated by the Communications Workers of America with AT&T, US West, and Lucent Technologies designed to upgrade the skills of existing employees to keep pace with emerging and changing technologies in the communications field have strong parallels to the technology heavy skills required of today's and the future's library employees (Nichols, 1996).

"Today the same set of skills no longer guarantees a worker his/her job for an entire career. . . . Our focus has shifted from job security to employment security. . . . The program offers workers a wide range of courses and programs to enhance their job skills and employability. . . . Nearly 50 percent of eligible workers have participated in Pathways programs. Union surveys also show that employees report a high degree of satisfaction with Pathways and consider the program one of their most important union-negotiated benefits." (Nichols, 1996, pp. 25–26)

Two other outstanding examples deserve mention as models for library work environments. Safe@Work is a joint labor management project dedicated to educating and assisting workers through a domestic violence awareness program sponsored by locals of Communication Workers of America, the International Brotherhood of Electrical Workers, and a major communications company (Safe@Work Coalition, n.d.). The company's employee assistance program works with union and management personnel to deliver targeted training to staff in jointly held sessions.

The State of Illinois Upward Mobility Program is a joint venture between the Illinois Department of Central Management Services and the American Federation of State, County, and Municipal Employees. Employees receive counseling to apprise them of career opportunities and to help them develop their career plans. Tuition subsidies to take applicable courses at various local schools are available to participants through the program (Illinois Department of Central Management Services, 2010).

Programs like Safe@Work and Upward Mobility are ideal for library workers, and the appeal of a jointly sponsored program provides an easy win for both labor and management: "Management and unions can agree on shared goals for training employees or work together as equal partners in designing a common project. . . . By establishing a common goal, management and unions can work toward ending a traditionally adversarial relationship. Effective workplace education programs often engender better workplace labor-management relations that can create an environment that is much more responsive to change than before. In the long run, this may be one of the most important benefits of workplace education programs and one of the most powerful inducements to get involved." (Conference Board, 1999, p. 9) The Conference Board (1999) report goes on to find that 98 percent of employers surveyed reported increases in both employee skills and economic benefits from workplace education programs (Conference Board, 1999, p. 6).

A 2001 study on the impact of joint labor management education programs on workers, employers, and unions found that "through joint labor management programs, unions and their partner employers can be a powerful source of training and education for employees of all types. . . . [A]s many as 30 percent of employers nationwide use unions, trade associations, or professional associations to provide training to their employees." (Van Buren, 2002, p. 11)

Some libraries are among these. Joint labor management programs at the various universities previously mentioned, whether they are in the trades or advisory councils like Yale's, also include the staff and faculty of university libraries. The State University of New York and New York State system and the United University Professors have negotiated to establish six joint committees, which include employment, safety and health, and professional development. The employment committee assists with retraining efforts for employees in at-risk positions, and the professional development committee oversees programs that provide supplemental support of employees' professional development activities, including research, course work, supervisor training, or attendance and participation in professional conferences. The safety and health committee provides targeted training to health and safety professionals (New York State and United University Professors, 2008). Also, the University of Connecticut's (2010) supervisor training for performance evaluation and merit purposes is conducted by a joint labor management team.

Trevor Dawes, circulation services director at Princeton University Library, recalled:

> Princeton University Library established a union management Library Education and Training Committee (LETC) through its collective bargaining agreement with AFSCME Local 956 over 10 years ago. The committee is composed of an equal number of union staff

and management members and sponsors a myriad of programs rang-ing from e-mail training to goal setting. The fact that members of the Princeton Library LETC are both professional and paraprofession-al indicates that LETC programs benefit all library staff members. LETC sponsors all sorts of programs from library tours for new and existing staff to hands on training on new library software to a buddy program for new library staff, the purpose of which acclimates new staff to the University and library environment. (Dawes, telephone conversation, August 12, 2010)

An example from public libraries can also be found in the nation's capital:

The Washington DC Public Library has participated in a joint labor management partnership with notable success. The public library was one participant in an effort featuring a number of city depart-ments and service groups. The partnership focused on employee mo-rale through labor-management collaboration and to promote con-tinuous learning. Three teams from the library received recognition from the partnership council for their efforts to improve space/use planning, update procedure manuals and improve employee recog-nition resulting in the creation of a new employee lounge and annu-al employee recognition ceremony. (U.S. Mayors, 2001; Partnering, 2002)

Joint programs such as these are powerful tools and should be cultivated by libraries as we move forward in challenging times.

REFERENCES

Brown University. (N.d.). "Collective Bargaining Agreement Between Brown University and United Service and Allied Workers—RI Facilities Management, October 13, 2006 to October 12, 2011." Retrieved from http://brown.edu/Administration/Human_Resources/downloads/USAW_RIContract.pdf

Conference Board. (1999). *Turning Skills into Profit: Economic Benefits of Workplace Education Programs*. New York, NY: Conference Board.

Illinois Department of Central Management Services. (2010). "Upward Mobility Program." Retrieved September 8, 2010, from www.state.il.us/cms/2_servicese_edu/umprgrm.htm

Indiana University. (2006). "Department of Physical Plant Apprenticeship Program." Retrieved from www.indiana.edu/~phyplant/apprenticeship.html

Indiana University. (2012). "Office of Environmental, Health, and Safety Management." Retrieved from www.ehs.indiana.edu/safety_committees.shtml

Michigan State University. (2009). "Health and Safety." Retrieved from www.msu.edu/~ctumsu/health.htm

New York State and United University Professors. (2008). "Joint Labor-Management Committees." Retrieved from www.nysuup.lmc.state.ny.us

Nichols, M. E. (1996, June–July). "CWA's Initiatives in Worker Training and Continuous Learning." *Community College Journal, 66*(6), 24–27.

"Partnering: DC Libraries Continue to Show the Way, Partnership Works!" (2002). *DCLMP Newsletter, 1*(2), 3.

Safe@Work Coalition. (N.d.). "Joint Labor/Management Domestic Violence Program." Retrieved from www.safeatworkcoalition.org/successstories/laborawareness.htm

Tomasko, E. S., & Dickinson, K. K. (1991). "The UAW-Ford Education, Development and Training Program." In L. A. Ferman, M. Hoyman, J. Cutcher-Gershenfeld, & E. J. Savoie (Eds.), *Joint Training Programs: A Union Management Approach to Preparing Workers for the Future* (pp. 55–70). Ithaca, NY: IRL Press.

UAW-Ford. (N.d.). "Education Development and Training Program." Retrieved from www.uawford.com/edtp.html

U.S. Bureau of Labor Statistics. (2010). "Economic News Release: Union Members Summary." Retrieved from www.bls.gov/news.release/union2.nr0.htm

U.S. Mayors. (2001, April 16). "Best Practice: Washington D.C. Mayor Holds Managers Accountable for Improving Labor-Management Cooperation." Retrieved from www.usmayors.org/bestpractices/usmayor01/dc_best_practice.asp

"U.S. Apprenticeship Development Links." (N.d.). Retrieved August 10, 2010, from www.zpdnc.com/links/apus.html

University of Connecticut. (2010). "UCPEA Supervisor Performance Evaluation and Merit Training." Retrieved August 10, 2010, from www.UCPEA_evaluation_training.ppt

Van Buren, M. E. (2002, November). *What Works in Workforce Development: An ASTD/AJLMEP Study of Joint Labor-Management Educational Programs.* Alexandria, VA: American Society for Training and Development.

Yale University. (2003, October 24). "Local 35 Issue #2 Item #2: Trades Helper—Externship Apprenticeship." Retrieved from www.yale.edu/hronline/labrelat/02_Local35_Trades.pdf

Yale University. (2009, April 14). "Yale and Unite Here Agree on Three-Year Contracts Nine Months Early." Retrieved from http://opa.yale.edu/news/article.aspx?id=6594

Yale University. (2010). "Working @ Yale." Retrieved from http://working.yale.edu/features/joint-labor-management-health-and-safety-committee-celeb

Part IV

Assessment

David Delbert Kruger and John Cochenour

chapter 17

Assessing and Ensuring the Transfer of Training

ORE THAN FORTY YEARS HAVE ELAPSED SINCE ALVIN Toffler (1970) wrote *Future Shock*, the book that prophesized how technological change could leave us perpetually alienated in our own working environments. With the passage of each decade since that publication, libraries have increasingly been reacting to technology and its incredible power to change how we do what we do, and with good reason. As Toffler (1980) later opined, "The illiterate of the 21st century will not be those who cannot read and write, but those who cannot learn, unlearn and relearn" (p. 12). Training functions as the tool of choice for perpetually equipping (and reequipping) library personnel to deal with new technologies, new resources, new users, and new methods for accomplishing the work of the library. Of course, none of this occurs without a cost. A recent report by the American Society of Training and Development estimated that annual training expenses have risen to about $955 per employee (Lee, 2010). How much of that investment actually benefits the workplace? When it comes to library investments, it is often easier to evaluate our efforts in, say, collection management as opposed to those in human resource development (HRD). Nevertheless, if the training libraries pay for is not effectively transferred to the library workplace, our HRD investments are as useful as buying, cataloging, and circulating books with the pages glued shut.

What Is Transfer of Training, and Why Is It Important to the Library Organization?

Transfer of training, by definition, is an individual's ability to take new knowledge, skills, and attitudes learned in a training environment and apply them over time to his or her actual working environment (Baldwin & Ford, 1988). Though often used synonymously with transfer of learning, transfer of training can be regarded as a subset of the former, focused more on tasks and particular skills (Leberman, McDonald, & Doyle, 2006). In theory, training transfer is a simple concept, encompassing the acquisition, application, and retention of training content. Unfortunately, research consistently shows that the content of any training program that will transfer immediately to the workplace is, at best, only around 30 to 40 percent (Saks & Belcourt, 2006). When long-term application and retention of training is considered, the percentage drops even lower, to around 10 percent by some estimates (Cheng & Ho, 2001).

Libraries in the twenty-first century cannot escape the need and expense for training any more than they can escape the changes that perpetually alter our profession. However, training investments with little or no transfer to the workplace are a waste of time and money, as well as a lost opportunity to effectively serve all of the library's stakeholders by improving the library organization. Libraries need to assess the training process to ensure that successful transfer follows our training investments.

HOW CAN TRANSFER OF TRAINING BE ASSESSED?

When it comes to assessment and evaluation of training transfer, the training expert Mary Broad (2005) invokes the axiom, "You don't get what you *expect,* you get what you *inspect*" (p. 113). The scope of a library's training-transfer assessment has to encompass far more than just performance results after training has taken place. Although the impulse is to limit this assessment to a training program or a trainee's posttraining performance, Broad and Newstrom (1992) propose evaluating training transfer from the chronological time perspectives of before, during, and after the actual training, as well as from the role perspectives of the trainee, the trainer, and the manager. Training transfer, therefore, cannot be regarded as a onetime episode; it must be regarded as an ongoing process. As components of that process, training programs and organizational environments need our critical eye as much as the posttraining performance of the trainee.

Hutchens and Burke (2007) have sought to distill theoretical research on training transfer into clear, practical applications for assessing it in the workplace. Their research, by examining previous studies, identified successful training-transfer characteristics for each training role, particularly when empirical research clearly supported a relationship between the presence of that characteristic and the occurrence of training transfer. Carnes (2010) has further categorized these transfer characteristics into the roles of the learner (as trainee), training design (including trainer, content, and delivery), and organizational environment and support (including key personnel in leadership positions).

It makes sense, practically and economically, to incorporate a critical assessment of trainees, training, and the library organization before any investment in training occurs, and to assess trainees, training programs, and the library organization during and after the training as part of that transfer assessment. The more successful transfer characteristics are present in each role, the greater is the likelihood that training will successfully transfer to the workplace.

ASSESSING THE TRAINEES TO ENSURE TRANSFER

Trainees, as learners in the training process, come in all shapes and sizes. Research supports that a trainee's cognitive ability (Colquitt, LePine, & Noe, 2000), self-confidence about performing the task (Carnes, 2010), and motivation levels (Nijman, Nijhof, Wognum, & Veldkamp, 2006) before training are all factors that contribute to training transfer. Care should be taken by the library organization to consider these characteristics when assessing trainees and planning training programs, with the understanding that not every trainee will approach and react to training in the same way. It may be possible that too much information in a given training program will overload some or all of the trainees involved, inevitably leading to loss of transfer. Other trainees may be confident about performing new skills in the safety of a training environment but experience fear and anxiety when it comes to transferring those skills to the "real" workplace. Research has shown that anxiety (Colquitt, LePine, & Noe, 2000) and negative affectivity (Machin & Fogarty, 2004) are significant predictors of unsuccessful transfer. Both of these can be detected and addressed by screening trainees ahead of time, to determine whether they are ready, psychologically and logistically, for training (Rossett, 1997).

Of course, trainee attitudes and perceptions about the training also play a role in successful transfer. A trainee's belief that new skills being trained will be useful and necessary for future job performance is a proven link to higher levels of transfer (Colquitt, LePine, & Noe, 2000). A trainee who values the outcomes that a training program provides will also yield higher transfer. A trainee's level of motivation to acquire new skills for the workplace directly contributes to successful transfer as well, particularly when that motivation is intrinsic (Kontoghiorghes, 2001). Strong identifications with workplace departments or units and commitment to the overall organization are also important trainee factors in predicting successful transfer (Kontoghiorghes, 2004).

Even with a diverse group of trainees, training transfer is strengthened when training environments foster extroversion (Barrick & Mount, 1991), specifically the ability to verbalize thoughts and feelings about tasks and their applications during the training (Carnes, 2010). The transfer benefits of extroversion are not lost on introverted trainees, who also benefit from training among extroverted trainees (Lemke, Leicht, & Miller, 1974). Extroversion stimulates cognitive sharing among all trainees, and this audible articulation increases the likelihood that training participants will benefit from the training process.

It is important to note that the absence of expected performance from a trainee does not always indicate the absence of training transfer. Not all performance needs can be addressed through training. Mager (1997) points out that if an employee can perform a trained skill in a life-or-death situation, the issue with that employee not otherwise performing that skill is not a training issue. It may be quite possible that a trainee may be unwilling to learn, because of a lack of motivation or possibly conditions in the working environment. In either case, these issues need to be addressed before training is implemented. Failure to do so can enable the trainee to falsely blame the trainer or the training for the lack of training transfer, even if training transfer has actually occurred.

ASSESSING THE TRAINING PROGRAM TO ENSURE TRANSFER

Factors in the training program also contribute to the success of training transfer. Just as instructional design has advanced to improve learning in the classroom, research supports the idea that these same elements in training programs lead to improved training transfer in the working environment.

Instructional librarians have long understood that teaching information literacy skills through active learning is far more productive than theoretically lecturing about these skills in front of a classroom. The same learning concepts apply to training sessions and training transfer (Burke, Sarpy, Smith-Crowe, Chan-Serafin, Salvador, & Islam, 2006). A good training session should provide opportunities to actively practice the skills being trained. New skills can fail if insufficient time is allowed for classroom practice, and trainees can grow discouraged if they do not immediately see desired results through new approaches in the workplace (Clarke, 2002). Giving the trainee the opportunity to learn from trial and error in the training environment develops the ability to positively cope with mistakes. Research has shown that training transfer is strengthened further when trainees are given feedback during these practice sessions (Hutchens & Burke, 2007).

Behavior modeling during the training is another component that enhances training transfer, whether the modeling is demonstrated in person or through learning technologies such as podcasts or compressed video (Taylor, Russ-Eft, & Chan, 2005). Modeling doesn't have to be entirely positive to be effective. Training that includes error-based examples, such as demonstrations showing ineffective behaviors or bad performances versus good performances, has also been shown to increase training transfer among participants (Joung, Hesketh, & Neal, 2006). Transfer increases even further when demonstrations emphasize key aspects of the desired performance. This is particularly important in training for complex library skills, such as conflict management at the circulation desk. Complex skills are harder to transfer than basic motor skills, such as desensitizing a book for checkout. To maximize transfer, complex skills should be broken down so that trainees understand the key components behind that skill and how those components relate to performing the skill as a whole. If the training for complex tasks is too general, it will be difficult for trainees to know how or when to use specific skills and behaviors, and the training will not effectively transfer to the workplace.

Relevancy of training content, or the perception thereof, is also a factor in training transfer (Axtell & Maitlis, 1997). This may seem like an obvious statement, but keep in mind that relevancy is not attained by merely placing training in the context of librarianship. What may be relevant to a cataloger in technical services may not be relevant to a reference librarian in public services, and vice versa. Even among catalogers, relevancy of training can vary considerably by job responsibilities and duties. In that regard, training should be tailored to reflect, whenever possible, relevancy to specific positions in the organization. To ensure effective transfer, it may be advantageous to break out separate training sessions that relevantly address similar positions and duties.

Does the training program clearly convey its goals and objectives? When goals and objectives of the training are clearly communicated to the trainee, training-transfer levels will be higher (Kontoghiorghes, 2001). Not only does this give the trainee context and meaning for the training tasks; it also clarifies the performance that is ultimately expected. Training transfer is even greater when goals and objectives are communicated to the trainee in advance of the actual training.

Finally, the implementation of self-management strategies near the end of the training session nurtures long-term transfer by giving trainees ownership in applying their new skills in the workplace. Of these self-management strategies, the two most strongly supported by research are goal setting and relapse prevention (Carnes, 2010).

ASSESSING THE ORGANIZATIONAL ENVIRONMENT TO ENSURE TRANSFER

John Donne's poetic observation that "no man is an island" certainly applies to the role of any organization in the transfer of new skills to the workplace. Training transfer does not occur in a vacuum of just the trainee and the training program. The library organization, particularly key personnel in supervisory or leadership positions, bear a certain responsibility. In fact, a number of HRD professionals believe that the organization is the most significant influence on whether transfer ultimately takes place (Tracey, Tannenbaum, & Kavanagh, 1995). Even leadership and staff not directly involved in the training still influence training transfer among trainees, for better or for worse. The support of leadership and the culture and climate of the organization, before and after the training, directly affect the degree to which trained skills are transferred from the training environment back to the workplace.

The nagging question, Why are we doing this training? is frequently attributed to trainees. However, leadership should provide the answer to that question long before a trainee ever asks and should assess their own level of support by reflecting on why they feel the training is necessary (Rossett, 1997). The responsibility for giving training meaning in the library must begin with library leadership, particularly as training ties to the organization's strategic planning. Higher levels of training transfer amongst trainees have been demonstrated when leadership effectively communicates the relationship between the training content and the strategic direction of the organization (Montesino, 2002). For effective transfer, leadership needs to explicitly share the purpose of any training throughout the organization and create a mutual understanding with trainees as to what the desired outcomes of the training are.

Peer behavior and attitudes are also powerful organizational catalysts in training transfer. Leadership should foster an environment that encourages communication among peers before training occurs (Chiaburu & Marinova, 2005). This communication helps articulate the value of the training, as well as ways the training might be applied in the workplace. Communication among peers after the training fosters a shared understanding of training challenges, successes, and further applications on the job. Coworker support has been shown to promote transfer even six months after a training program has been completed (Hawley & Barnard, 2005).

A negative working environment can obviously hinder successful training transfer (Kontoghiorghes, 2001). When key personnel, including immediate supervisors, take a passive or antagonistic attitude toward any change brought about by a training program, their approach will undermine training transfer in the workplace. Trainees will naturally be discouraged to retain new skills or approaches from training if they feel it contradicts the values of the organization or department they serve. Failure by leadership to reinforce or reward trained behavior after the training also undermines the process. However, simply silencing negative attitudes and behaviors does not enhance transfer. Training transfer thrives when leadership actively shows support for the training (Foxon, 1997). Specific actions, such as discussing the training with trainees, participating in the training in some visible form, and providing encouragement as a training coach all improve training transfer, not to mention trainee morale during uncertain times of change (Carnes, 2010).

If the support by library leadership is an effective carrot for training transfer, accountability by the same leadership can be regarded as an effective stick (Taylor, Russ-Eft, & Chan, 2005). Training programs need follow-up to ensure long-term maintenance of new skills, and organizational accountability holds trainees responsible for applying what they learn. Accountability can be implemented through positive or negative performance reviews, or simply requiring that trainees provide a posttraining report on their training experiences and applications to the workplace. Accountability for training transfer also falls on library leadership. Leadership should clearly understand the skills being trained and be able to identify appropriate changes in job performance as a result of the training.

Perhaps the most important factor in training transfer is the opportunity to perform trained skills in the workplace, preferably as soon as the training is completed. Leadership has the power to provide and facilitate these opportunities in the workplace, and it is certainly in the organization's best interest to do so. In several studies, this factor was found to have the highest influence on training transfer. Conversely, research found that the reduction or absence of on-the-job practice was the greatest barrier to effective training transfer (Clarke, 2002).

Conclusion

If transfer of training occurred every time training occurred, this chapter would be entirely unnecessary. Libraries would receive a full return on all HRD investments, maximizing human resource efficiency and potential across the organization. In reality, though, libraries must understand that the presence of training does not automatically lead to the transfer of training. Without effective transfer in the short and long term, the already-limited time, money, and energy libraries spend on training programs are wasted. In today's economic climate, anything perceived as a bad investment tends to quickly lose support, financially and politically. But the greater loss for libraries is the opportunity to truly develop and equip the library organization to take advantage of an ever-evolving profession, whether the new work involves integrating metadata into the catalog or answering reference questions using Facebook. No matter how much a library trains, or how much it spends on training, it will never maximize its return on that investment unless transfer of training truly occurs. Assessing training transfer throughout the training process is a giant step toward ensuring that all stakeholders in the library will ultimately get their money's worth.

REFERENCES

Axtell, C. M., & Maitlis, S. (1997). "Predicting Immediate and Longer-Term Transfer of Training." *Personnel Review, 26*(3), 201–213.

Baldwin, T., & Ford, J. K. (1988). "Transfer of Training: A Review and Directions for Future Research." *Personnel Psychology, 41*(2), 63–105.

Barrick, M. R., & Mount, M. K. (1991). "The Big Five Personality Dimensions and Job Performance: A Meta-Analysis." *Personnel Psychology, 44*, 1–26.

Broad, M. L. (2005). *Beyond Transfer of Training: Engaging Systems to Improve Performance.* San Francisco: Wiley.

Broad, M. L., & Newstrom, J. W. (1992). *Transfer of Training: Action-Packed Strategies to Ensure Payoff from Training Investments.* Reading, MA: Addison-Wesley.

Burke, M. J., Sarpy, S. A., Smith-Crowe, K., Chan-Serafin, S., Salvador, R. O., & Islam, G. (2006). "Relative Effectiveness of Worker Safety and Health Training Methods." *American Journal of Public Health, 96*(2), 315–324.

Carnes, B. (2010). *Making Learning Stick.* Alexandria, VA: ASTD Press.

Cheng, E. W. L., & Ho, D. C. K. (2001). "A Review of Transfer of Training Studies in the Past Decade." *Personnel Review, 30*(1), 102–118.

Chiaburu, D. S., & Marinova, S. V. (2005). "What Predicts Skill Transfer? An Exploratory Study of Goal Orientation, Training Self-Efficacy and Organizational Supports." *International Journal of Training and Development, 9,* 110–123.

Clarke, N. (2002). "Job/Work Environment Factors Influencing Training Effectiveness Within a Human Service Agency: Some Indicative Support for Baldwin and Ford's Transfer Climate Construct." *International Journal of Training and Development, 6*(3), 146–162.

Colquitt, J. A., LePine, J. A., & Noe, R. A. (2000). "Toward an Integrative Theory of Training Motivation: A Meta-Analytic Path Analysis of 20 Years of Research." *Journal of Applied Psychology, 85*(5), 678–707.

Foxon, M. (1997). "The Influence of Motivation to Transfer, Action Planning, and Manager Support on the Transfer Process." *Performance Improvement Quarterly, 10*(2), 42–63.

Hawley, J. D., & Barnard, J. K. (2005). "Work Environment Characteristics and Implications for Training Transfer: A Case Study of the Nuclear Power Industry." *Human Resource Development International, 8*(1), 65–80.

Hutchens, H. M., & Burke, L. A. (2007). "Identifying Trainers' Knowledge of Training Transfer Research Findings: Closing the Gap Between Research and Practice." *International Journal of Training and Development, 11*(4), 236–264.

Kontoghiorghes, C. (2001). "Factors Affecting Training Effectiveness in the Context of the Introduction of New Technology: A US Case Study." *International Journal of Training and Development, 5*(4), 248–260.

Kontoghiorghes, C. (2004). "Reconceptualizing the Learning Transfer Conceptual Framework: Empirical Validation of a New Systemic Model." *International Journal of Training and Development, 8*(3), 210–221.

Leberman, S., McDonald, L., & Doyle, S. (2006). *The Transfer of Learning: Participants' Perspectives of Adult Education and Training.* Surrey, UK: Gower.

Lee, J. (2010). "Design of Blended Training for Transfer into the Workplace." *British Journal of Educational Technology, 41*(2), 181–198.

Lemke, E. A., Leicht, K. L., & Miller, J. C. (1974). "Role of Ability and Extroversion in Concept Attainment of Individuals Trained in Heterogeneous or Homogeneous Personality Groups." *Journal of Educational Research*, 67(5), 202–204.

Machin, M. A., & Fogarty, G. J. (2004). "Assessing the Antecedents of Transfer Intentions in a Training Context." *International Journal of Training and Development*, 8(3), 222–236.

Mager, R. F. (1997). *Analyzing Performance Problems* (3rd ed.). Atlanta, GA: Center for Effective Performance.

Montesino, M. U. (2002). "A Descriptive Study of Some Organizational-Behavior Dimensions at Work in the Dominican Republic: Implications for Management Development and Training." *Human Resource Development International*, 5(4), 393–410.

Nijman, D.-J. J. M., Nijhof, W. J., Wognum, A. A. M., & Veldkamp, B. P. (2006). "Exploring Differential Effects of Supervisor Support on Transfer of Training." *Journal of European Industrial Training*, 30(7), 529–549.

Rossett, A. (1997). "That Was a Great Class, But . . ." *Training and Development*, 51(7), 18–24.

Saks, A. M., & Belcourt, M. (2006). "An Investigation of Training Activities and Transfer of Training in Organizations." *Human Resource Management*, 45(4), 629–648.

Taylor, P. J., Russ-Eft, D. F., & Chan, D. W. L. (2005). "A Meta-Analytic Review of Behavior Modeling Training." *Journal of Applied Psychology*, 90(4), 692–709.

Toffler, A. (1970). *Future Shock*. New York, NY: Random House.

Toffler, A. (1980). *The Third Wave*. New York, NY: Bantam.

Tracey, J. B., Tannenbaum, S. I., & Kavanagh, M. J. (1995). "Applying Trained Skills on the Job: The Importance of the Work Environment." *Journal of Applied Psychology*, 80(2), 239–252.

Contributors

Elizabeth Fuseler Avery is currently coordinator of collection development at the University of North Texas in Denton. She is a past president of the Mountain Plains Library Association and the International Association of Aquatic and Marine Science Libraries and Information Centers. She has been active in staff development and training for more than twenty years and is a past editor of *Staff Development: A Practical Guide* (2001). Her research interests include assessment of instruction and reference and bibliographic analysis.

Julia Blixrud is currently the assistant executive director, scholarly communication, for the Association of Research Libraries. Her research interests are cooperative programs, serials, technical standards, library assessment, leadership and organizational development, intellectual property, and scholarly communication.

Chad F. Boeninger is the head of reference and business librarian at Ohio University's Alden Library. He is the creator of the *Business Blog,* a popular resource for business researchers all over. He has presented and written about a variety of Web 2.0 and library technology tools such as wikis, blogs, instant messaging, open source software, podcasting, gaming, and social software. He is passionate about using technology as a means of personalizing the library and highlighting the value of librarians as essential resources. Chad shares his thoughts and ideas about libraries and technology on his personal blog, *Library Voice.*

Raynna Bowlby is an associate of Library Management Consulting (LMC). She provides program reviews and organizational assessments for academic libraries and guides libraries of various types in strategic planning and the development of assessment plans. She regularly consults with the Association of Research Libraries to enable librarians to effectively use data obtained from assessment initiatives and user surveys such as LibQUAL+. She also assists libraries with change management and leadership development and with LMC's core business, library cost-analysis studies. Bowlby is an adjunct faculty member for the Simmons College Graduate School of Library and Information Science, where she teaches Principles of Management. Previously, she was organizational and staff development officer for the Brown University Library. In addition to her MSLS from Simmons GSLIS, Bowlby has a master's degree in business administration from the University of Rhode Island.

Steven Carr has held a number of positions at the Arlington (VA) Public Library, where he currently manages a combined branch library and retail store, as well as supervises the law library in the County Detention Center. Prior to this, Steve owned a retail store and was the executive director of the Lancaster County Library in Pennsylvania. Steve received his MS degree from the University of Illinois and has been certified as a public manager by the George Washington University and the Metropolitan Washington Council of Governments. He is also among the first librarians to become a LEED-accredited professional by the U.S. Green Building Council. In addition to LLAMA committee work with ALA, Carr also serves on education committees for the U.S. Green Building Council. He is a sustainability expert, library facilities designer, and avid quilter. He currently lives in Fairfax, VA.

John Cochenour is a professor of education in the Professional Studies Department at the University of Wyoming. He is a combat veteran of the United States Marine Corps and has taught and published in the areas of information use and access, distance education, instructional design and development, change theory, and visual literacy. Cochenour holds a PhD and two master's degrees from the University of Oklahoma.

Myntha Cuffy is a reference and instruction librarian at the University of Iowa Libraries. Her research interests include the pedagogy of research methods in MLS programs, curriculum development for online learning environments, and organizational structures in academic libraries.

Lila Daum Fredenburg has served as director for administrative services at Rutgers University Libraries since 2007. Prior to that she held a similar position at Florida State University and served as human resources librarian at Princeton University Libraries and Indiana University Libraries. Before obtaining her MLIS from the University of Illinois at Urbana-Champaign in 1998, she practiced labor and employment law in Ohio and Illinois. She has served on several committees in LLAMA and was elected chair of the Human Resources Section from 2007 to 2008. She contributed the chapter on labor relations activity in academic libraries to *Human Resource Management in Today's Academic Library,* published in 2004 by Libraries Unlimited.

Joan Giesecke is the dean of libraries, University of Nebraska–Lincoln Libraries. She joined UNL in 1987 and became dean in 1996. Prior to this, she was the associate dean for collections and services. She has held positions at George Mason University in Fairfax, VA; Prince George's County Memorial System; and the American Health Care Association. She received a doctorate in public administration (DPA) from George Mason University, an MLS from the University of Maryland, a master's degree in management from Central Michigan University, and a BA in economics from State University of New York at Buffalo. Giesecke's research interests include leadership, organizational decision making, and management skills, and she publishes extensively in these areas. She also teaches courses in leadership at the library school at Simmons College.

Robyn Huff-Eibl is the team leader for Access and Information Services at the University of Arizona Libraries. She has worked at the libraries for the past twenty years, holding a variety of positions on several different teams. As team leader for Access and Information Services, she oversees reference services, circulation and billing, express retrieval, equipment lending, interlibrary loan support, and user services as they relate to library space. Huff-Eibl has participated in several Living the Future conferences and cochaired the most recent conference in 2008, "Living the Future 7: Transforming Libraries through Collaboration" (www.library.arizona.edu/conferences/ltf/2008).

Elaine Z. Jennerich is director of organization development and training for the University of Washington Libraries. She is the author or coauthor of articles about staff development in *College and Research Libraries News* and *OD Practitioner*, as well as coauthor of two editions of *The Reference Interview as Creative Art*. Her presentations and copresentations at the Association of College and Research Libraries and OD Network national meetings have included workshops about new employee orientation, dealing with change, and appreciative inquiry. She earned her PhD in library science from the University of Pittsburgh.

Carol A. Kochan has worked in libraries for twenty-five years. She has been the coordinator of interlibrary loan services at Utah State University for sixteen years. She has an MLS from the University of Arizona.

David Delbert Kruger is the agricultural research librarian at the University of Wyoming. Originally an instructional librarian, he spent seven years of his career in library administration, and continues to be a trainer with the United States Army Reserves. Kruger holds a master's degree in library and information science from the University of Missouri-Columbia and a master's degree in English from Kansas State University.

Beth McNeil is professor and associate dean for academic affairs in the Purdue University Libraries, where she is responsible for public services, collections, and scholarly communication. Before joining Purdue in 2007, McNeil was associate dean of libraries at University of Nebraska–Lincoln. She received an MS in library and information science from the University of Illinois at Urbana-Champaign. She is the coauthor of *Fundamentals of Library Supervision*, with Joan Giesecke (2005 and 2010), and coeditor of *Human Resource Management in Today's Academic Library*, with Janice Simmons-Welburn (2004) and *Advocacy, Outreach & the Nation's Academic Libraries: A Call for Action*, with William Welburn and Janice Welburn (2010).

Lisa A. Oberg is the head of outreach services for the Health Sciences Library and former coordinator of staff development and training at the University of Washington

Libraries. After receiving her master's degree in librarianship from the University of Washington, she worked in a variety of capacities, ranging from managing a public service desk to working closely with basic science and bench-top researchers. Her staff development activities have included teaching, mentoring, and coaching for customer service excellence; employee morale; team building; and designing and planning events to build workplace community.

Dorothy Marie Persson is currently the psychology and education liaison librarian at the University of Iowa Libraries. Her research interests are in the areas of reference and user instruction. She holds a PhD in higher education from the University of Iowa, an MLS in library science from Indiana University, and a BA in political science and economics from Ohio University.

Linda Plunket is the associate university librarian for graduate and research services at Boston University. She works closely with the university librarian and the other two associate university librarians to formulate strategy and implement plans. She manages six branch libraries and two departments. Plunket is responsible for staff and organizational development and library assessment. She was formerly the training and development coordinator for the libraries at Boston University and the head of the Pickering Educational Resources Library in the School of Education. She has a master's degree in library and information science from Rutgers University and a master's in oceanography from the University of Maine.

Andrea Wigbels Stewart holds the position of associate university librarian for administration, development, and human resources at the Estelle and Melvin Gelman Library, George Washington University, Washington, DC. She received her master's degree in education and human development from George Washington's Graduate School of Education and Human Development. Active in the American Library Association since 1997, she has served as the Library Leadership and Management Association's Human Resources Section secretary and cochair of the Staff Development Committee.

Maureen Sullivan is an organization development consultant whose practice focuses on the delivery of consulting and education services to libraries and other information organizations. Her career history includes twelve years as the human resources administrator in the libraries at the University of Maryland and at Yale University. She is a member of the faculty for the annual ACRL/Harvard Graduate School of Education's Leadership Institute for Academic Librarians and a professor of practice in the PhD/Managerial Leadership in the Information Professions program at the Simmons College Graduate School of Library and Information Science. She was president of the Library Administration and Management Association for the 1988–1989 term.

Julie Todaro is dean of library services at Austin Community College. Her research interests include staff development in general and, specifically, management, customer service, and leadership and mentoring.

Jeanne F. Voyles received her master's degree in library science from the University of Arizona. Her first professional position was head loan librarian in the loan department at the University of Arizona Library. When the University of Arizona Library moved to a team-based organization, she was selected as team leader of the Materials Access Team, a position she held from 1993 to June 2002, when she was appointed to lead a new team in the library, the Document Delivery Team. Voyles is active on a national level and has been appointed and led national committees with a focus on leadership and management and interlibrary loan. She has presented and published primarily in the areas of interlibrary loan, process improvement, staff development, and customer service.

Carlette Washington-Hoagland is coordinator of assessment and staff development at the University of Iowa Libraries, where she has served in various capacities for thirteen years. Her research interests include staff development, usability testing, service quality, faculty-librarian collaboration, engagement, sexual harassment, and retention. Previous experience includes serving as a research analyst and trial consultant for a litigation firm and as a marketing researcher at a major U.S. appliance manufacturer. She earned an MA in library and information science from the University of Iowa, an MS in sociology from Iowa State University, and a BS in social work from Southern University, A&M Colleges.

Sandra J. Weingart has been a librarian for eighteen years, the last fourteen of them in the reference department at Utah State University's Merrill-Cazier Library. She earned a BS in animal science from the University of Connecticut and an MLS from the University of Kentucky.

Carol T. Zsulya is currently head of collection management and the business and economics librarian at Cleveland State University. She received a bachelor of arts degree from Ursuline College, Cleveland, Ohio, and an MSLS degree from Case Western Reserve University, Cleveland, Ohio. Using her extensive industry background and experience, she works closely with the Nance College of Business Administration dean, associate deans, faculty, students, and the Greater Cleveland business community to advance the mission of the college. Carol is also active in the Ohio library community as a member of three OhioLINK committees relative to collection management. She participated in the Charleston Conference in November 2010 as a panel member in two programs: Changing Operations of Academic Libraries and Do Humanities & Social Sciences E-Books Get Used?

Index

Page numbers in bold refer to figures and tables.

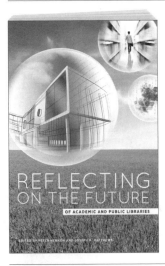

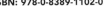